Together in Time

A FAMILY STORY

EUGENE FAGNANO

Gotham Books

30 N Gould St.
Ste. 20820, Sheridan, WY 82801
https://gothambooksinc.com/

Phone: 1 (307) 464-7800

© 2024 *Eugene Fagnano*. All rights reserved.

No part of this book may be reproduced, stored in a retrieval system, or transmitted by any means without the written permission of the author.

Published by Gotham Books (July 10, 2024)

ISBN: 979-8-3303-3322-6 (H)
ISBN: 979-8-3303-3320-2 (P)
ISBN: 979-8-3303-3321-9 (E)

Because of the dynamic nature of the Internet, any web addresses or links contained in this book may have changed since publication and may no longer be valid.

The views expressed in this work are solely those of the author and do not necessarily reflect the views of the publisher, and the publisher hereby disclaims any responsibility for them.

Table of Contents

Dedication i
Acknowledgements ii
Foreword iii
Introduction iv
The Beginning 1
World War 1 & The Years That Followed 9
Home, Sweet Home 16
My Siblings 23
The White Castle Years 65
Growing Up During Wartime 69
The Post War Years 72
Meeting The Love Of My Life 73
The Crisis 79
"Neither Rain, Nor Sleet" 82
The Tragedy 91
Life Without Papa 93
Life on Park Avenue 95
The Fagnano Boys and Their Antics 98
Political Life 107
My Years as a Pressman 111
Our Children 121
Through the Years 133
Epilogue 138

Dedication

This book is dedicated to my mother and father. They brought me into this world and raised me and my siblings with their love and care during the most difficult of times. They made sacrifices that only love and faith could endure. The years may have stolen some of my memories but I have been blessed to have retained enough of them in order to share this with you. I feel obligated to preserve for future generations as many memories as my aging mind can recall.

Acknowledgements

My co-author and youngest daughter, Cindy Petrocelli, with whom I live, has given me both the opportunity and assistance I needed to write this book. When I found it frustrating and difficult she encouraged me to continue. She assisted me with the tasks of formatting and researching required. My older daughter, Debbie Fagnano, who lives in metro New Orleans, also helped with advice, researching, and her knowledge of editing and formatting. My nephew, Michael Verina, contributed and shared many of the photos that were used. My sisters, Dolores Deery and Rose Stigliano helped me with the timeline and sequence of events. I hope my story is worthy of all those who have helped me in this endeavor.

Foreword

    To a skilled writer, words can either make a statement or they can impart knowledge and real emotions. I do not consider myself a skilled writer, and as I search for the words to express my final thoughts I am reminded of my original intent in the writing of this book. I have attempted to put into words the life experience of one family and their struggles, hopes, and dreams for a brighter future in a very troubled world. I will be grateful knowing that I achieved my goal if readers could derive from these words the knowledge that good friends may come and go, but families are forever, and good fortune is enjoyed most when shared with others.

Introduction

Blessed with longevity by the grace of God, I have been given the opportunity to pass on the legacy of the Fagnano family. Hopefully, our traditions will be carried on by the many children, grandchildren, and great-grandchildren we now enjoy. This is the story of nine lives, and though they each followed different paths in life they stayed united in their determination to remain a cohesive and bonded family. Their struggles through the early years were met with a never ending optimism for a brighter future as long as they were together. World War II put a temporary hold on their quest. The end of the war burst through like a ray of sunshine. They were then rewarded for their faith and perseverance with many years of unparalleled joy that soon became the envy of the community.

Thus began the legacy of the Fagnano family……nine children, nine lives, nine stories.

The Beginning

We are all on this earth for a predestined amount of time. For my family, the clock was set in motion when a group of immigrants from the tiny village of Valsinni, Italy, departed from a port in Naples, Italy, aboard the SS Alberta, bound for America. They arrived in New York on June 22, 1904. Among the passengers was the family of Fabiano Fagnano, my grandfather. He had entered the United States some time earlier with several other friends and relatives, hoping to earn enough money to return to Italy and bring his family back to America. Tragically, he lost a leg in an accident at the mill where he worked in Niles, Ohio, and would be unable to return to Italy. However, he had earned enough money to send for his wife, Carmella Rosa, and their five children, Maria, Carmella, my father Francesco, Rocco and Andrew. Upon arriving, a group of the other travelers from Valsinni stayed in New Jersey. The family of Fabiano went on to reunite with him in Niles, Ohio. Many of our relatives had already settled there, and they were happy to greet Carmella and her children. With many jobs readily available in the steel mill and on the railroad, the town was flourishing. Fabiano had a home waiting for the arrival of his family. He and his wife, Carmella, accepted boarders to help pay for expenses. Like most other families in town they had a small vegetable garden and canned all their own produce for the cold winters. Every home had a special room for their dry sausages, canned food, jellies and dried peppers. They baked their own bread, and food in general was plentiful. Some of the other settlers had opened tailor shops and small businesses, and quite a few were bricklayers and builders. They often used their talents to assist each other with building their homes. Others, more ambitious, took advantage of the times and turned to, "bootlegging," and "moonshining," for a living. My father's brothers, James and Sam, were born there, followed by a sister, Dora. The family grew and prospered. The settlers from Valsinni had become a large community in Niles, and among them the Fagnano family multiplied into a large and well known clan.

Fabiano Fagnano with sons Sam (left) and Franceso, my father, (right)

Fagnano family settlers in Niles, Ohio

Papa Frank & Mama Rose

Papa Frank

Papa Frank

My father, Francesco, was born in Valsinni, Italy, on February 12, 1894, son of Fabiano Fagnano and Carmella Rosa Zaccone (Cozzo.) He joined two older sisters, Maria and Carmella, and was followed by two brothers, Rocco and Andrew. His father was a farmer, who, seeking a better life for his family, sailed to America. He joined relatives and friends in Niles, Ohio, and looked for work and a home to house his wife and children. He had planned to return to Italy to bring them back to America but was unable to do so. He had lost a leg in an accident at the mill where he worked and was unable to travel. So my grandmother, with her five children, boarded the SS Alberta and sailed for America. My father, at the age of ten, arrived with them in New York on June 22, 1904, they moved on to settle in with my grandfather in Niles, Ohio. Three more of my father's siblings were born there, James, Sam and Dora. My father had very little education and at the age of sixteen began working as a barber's apprentice, giving haircuts in the basement of his mother's house. Papa met and married his first love, Rose Rotundo, in 1914. They lived with his mother in her boarding house in Niles for a while, with Papa working as a barber and Mama helping her mother-in-law with the household chores. Then Papa opened a small barbershop with his brother, Andrew, and he was able to buy his first home.

Mama Rose

Mama Rose

My mother, Rose Rotundo, was born in Niles, Ohio, on October 31, 1898, daughter of Gennaro Rotundo and Ninziada Scheero Cirgillina. She was raised in Niles, along with her brother, Frank, and half-brother, Anthony. (Her mother had divorced her first husband and remarried, taking the surname, Rotundo.) Mama was well educated and had come from what was considered to be a middle-class family. As a young girl she learned to play the church organ. She had a fairly cultured childhood and at the age of fifteen met my father. It was the first love for both of them. My mother was the picture of innocence and my father was "movie star" handsome. Her mother was reluctant to approve of their courtship because of their age. Mama was barely sixteen. At the time however, it was common to marry young. After they were married on September 19, 1914, Mama and Papa moved into his mother's house and began what would become the challenging task of raising a family. My grandmother had taken in boarders to help with expenses and my mother took on the responsibilities of making their lunches every day, along with doing the household chores. It was not easy for the young bride but she never complained. Anxious to start a family, she and Papa accepted her father's offer of financial assistance and they bought their first home nearby. With Papa working steadily in the barbershop, Mama's dream of having a big family was about to become a reality.

Mama & Papa

World War 1 & The Years That Followed

Suddenly, World War I began and with it the country prospered. While most of the men went off to war there were plenty of jobs for those left behind. Mama and Papa had begun to grow their family with the birth of my sister, Adeline, on July 9, 1915, followed by my brother, Albert, on Nov. 9, 1917. My father, now with two children, was not called to duty. His business flourished. He was able to buy a new car and he moved his growing family to a bigger home nearby. As the war ended, the good times began and Mama and Papa continued to grow their family. The next few years were cause to rejoice while families grew and prospered. Any event was an excuse for a celebration - anniversaries, birthdays, baptisms, weddings or any other special occasion. My father was a talented violinist. My sister, Adeline, learned to play the piano and my brother, Albert, played the clarinet. As they became older, they were often called on to entertain on special occasions. Most of my uncles all played one instrument or another so there was always music and dancing. There was an abundance of homemade wine and liquor, and the women thrived on their cooking talents, always trying to outdo one another with their secret recipes. The people were working hard and enjoying life in general.

Then the clouds began to appear and the festivities became less frequent. The wartime prosperity had disappeared and people began to feel the effects of the slow down. Jobs were becoming scarce and there was no relief in sight. My brother, Raymond, was born on January 12, 1921. With his business falling off, my father began looking for a solution. People were leaving Niles to look for work in the bigger cities, but his brothers and sisters were determined to wait it out, hoping for a recovery. There wasn't enough business to sustain two barbers with their small shop so Papa's brother, Andrew, decided to seek employment elsewhere. My father was struggling to stay in business and was becoming desperate. He had a cousin, Dominic D'Alessandro, living in North Bergen, New Jersey, who had also migrated from Valsinni. They corresponded regularly, and often compared lifestyles. Dominic was a tailor by trade and at that time was earning a comfortable living. He convinced my father that there were better opportunities in New Jersey and encouraged him to consider moving there. After much soul-searching and against the wishes of family and friends, he decided to look into the possibility of making the move. Willing to try anything to improve his situation, he made a brief trip to New Jersey, and after a short stay decided it was worth a try. He returned to Ohio to settle all of his affairs and make arrangements for the big move. He rented out our home and made all the arrangements for a permanent departure. My father and mother, with their children, Adeline, Albert and Raymond, all boarded a train and left for New Jersey, leaving all family ties behind. My father set up a barber chair in the rear of his cousin's tailor shop and began a two-year struggle to support his family, which had now increased by one more with the birth of my sister, Rita, on August 8, 1923. It soon became obvious they weren't making any better progress in New Jersey than they had in Ohio. Finally, in desperation, Papa gave up and decided to return to Niles. Upon arriving there he found that nothing there had changed. Jobs were still scarce and they joined the plight of the rest of the townspeople there in a quest for survival. Mama accepted it all in stride, one of her greatest virtues was faith. My mother bore the burden of feeding and caring for her growing brood with complete faith in my father's ability to somehow resolve our dilemma and continue to provide for the family she had dreamed of. At least they had their own home and managed to cope with the stresses of the times. Besides her household chores, Mama kept busy canning her home grown produce, and by baking, sewing and dressmaking for a few extra dollars.

Regardless of the hardships, our family endured and continued to grow. My brother Anthony, was born on August 21, 1925. When the clock began ticking for me on January 18, 1928, I'm not sure my arrival was met with much enthusiasm, considering the economic conditions at that time. However, Italians traditionally believed in large families, so I like to think that I was a welcomed addition to our family. The fact that three more sisters were born after me gave credibility to my belief that our births were planned and welcomed.

However, by the time of the birth of my sister, Dolores, on March 30, 1930, our situation had become critical. We were about to lose our home.

Our house on Summit Avenue in Niles, Ohio

Having a wife and seven children to support, my father had few options left. Refusing to accept defeat, he made the difficult decision to go ahead and once more explore his options in New Jersey before moving his whole family again. He had only my sister, Adeline, leave high school and join him. He set up shop again in the rear of his cousin's tailor shop and was determined to succeed. There was no turning back now.

Papa became acquainted with the owner of a dress shop who offered to hire my sister, Adeline, to work as a seamstress. She began working as soon as she arrived. It was difficult work for one so young, but she learned quickly, and in a short time was promoted to forelady. Feeling guilty about taking Adeline out of school where she was an honor student, my father had her enrolled in a night school for a small fee so she could get her diploma. She studied business administration, typing and bookkeeping. Later in life, she used these skills to run her husband's business and go on to a career in teaching.

My father was doing well with his barber chair in the back of the tailor shop. With Adeline and my father both working they earned enough money to send for my brother, Albert. He left school and joined my sister at the dress shop, which by today's standards would be called a "sweatshop". He earned fourteen cents an hour. Their meager salaries were still barely enough to sustain them. Not yet able to afford an apartment, they lived in the basement of our cousin's home for a short time. They finally managed to save enough money to send for the rest of us in Ohio. Once again, my mother packed all our belongings and we were off to New Jersey, this time for good. In the years that followed, Mama was lonely and homesick and would often cry for all she had left behind.

Meanwhile, my father was still working from the rear of the tailor shop and had gained a respectable following. He found rooms for us in a two-family house nearby. It was here that my sister, Rose, was born on February 28, 1933. Our family was continuing to grow. And I began attending school in the First Grade. The future was beginning to look a little brighter.

My father decided it was time to move on in his business. He eventually found a small storefront for rent a short distance from the tailor shop and opened his own barbershop, Artistic Barber. We moved to another apartment in North Bergen for a short stay. He was doing well with his own shop now, his steady customers followed him, and soon he bought a second chair and hired a young man, Fabian Zaccone, to help him. Fabian's family also came from Valsinni and they were distant cousins. Fabian was studying art and worked part-time with my father to pay his way through school. We were beginning to enjoy a more normal existence. Once more, my mother set up a household. We even had a little dog, the first time we had a pet. This felt like a real home now. The situation in Ohio was improving and my grandmother began sending us care packages. We waited eagerly for their arrival because they contained canned fruits and vegetables, dried sausages and homemade cookies. It was like old times again. Then one day my mother received a telegram. My father's mother was very ill and his family suggested he make a quick visit to see her. He boarded a bus for Ohio as the quickest way to get there. Somewhere in Pennsylvania the bus ran off the road and turned over. Among the many people injured, my father suffered a broken ankle and was sent to the nearest hospital. My father belonged to the

Knights of Columbus and always wore his pin. Ironically, one of the rescuers noticed his pin and said he also was a Knight. He took a special interest in my father's welfare and contacted my mother. He arranged for her to come to Pennsylvania and she was able to visit my father in the hospital. That Knight's kindness was never forgotten and many years later it inspired me and my three brothers to join the Knights of Columbus in memory of my father. After a short stay in the hospital, Papa returned home to the welcoming arms of his family. Now Mama had a difficult task ahead. She nursed and consoled my father back to health while still caring for our growing family. Papa would be unable to work for some time while his leg was still in a brace. In an extreme gesture of compassion, young Fabian agreed to work at the barbershop until my father was able to return. Fabian later became a famous artist and would forever be remembered for his kindness.

After Papa returned to work we moved to an apartment not far from the barbershop, and directly across the street from a school. There was a Jewish synagogue next door to our home. Having never seen rabbis in their full attire, and with their long hair and beards I was somewhat frightened by their appearance. I could hear them chanting in prayer on their holy days and it was quite a while before I understood it was a religion and nothing to be afraid of. There was also a firehouse on the corner of our street and I became very friendly with the firemen who lived there. They were very kind to me and I became their mascot. They would let me sit in the driver's seat of the fire engine and ring the big silver bell mounted on the bumper. After polishing the bell they would give me candy bars. Now and then they would give me gifts of clothing or toys. I spent many hours at that firehouse.

It was in this apartment that my mother, at home in her bedroom, gave birth to my sister, Frances, on Thanksgiving Day, November 27, 1934, while we were having dinner in the dining room. As destiny would have it, Frances would be the last child to join our family. There were some who questioned the wisdom of having so many children but it was never an issue with my mother. She had complete faith in my father's ability to provide for them. She and my father had vowed faithfully to each other to have a large family.

Not long before this, Daniel Verina, whose family we had known from Ohio, began courting my oldest sister, Adeline. Dan had also migrated from Ohio and was living with his uncle in a nearby town. He and Adeline had known about each other since childhood, but he was from a different part of town in Niles and they never saw much of each other. His father was a very strict man, often abusive. While still in his teens, Dan left home and moved to New Jersey, living first in a boarding house for a while, then moving in with a cousin. He became a self-taught mechanic. When he found out through a friend that we were also living in New Jersey he visited my father at his barbershop. Because he was a young man living alone, my father invited him to our home for supper. After a few more visits he asked my father's permission to date my sister Adeline. My father gave his consent and soon Dan Verina became part of our family.

Dan with his pet Monkey

Mama Rose & Papa Frank, Fairview, NJ Home

Home, Sweet Home

Now, finding it more difficult to find rooms for such a large family, my father decided it was time to buy our own home. A friend in the real estate business showed him a home on North 8th Street in the nearby town of Fairview, a few miles from his barbershop. The house was in a quiet neighborhood, a very rural area with plenty of open spaces. When we first saw it, it seemed like we were moving to the country. This would be the final move we would make together as a family. There we were, Mama and Papa with their five daughters and four sons, all living in a house with three small bedrooms and only one bathroom. The large basement had a storage room where coal was delivered through a window. The basement was equipped with a sink, stove and refrigerator. In the years that followed I was able to renovate the basement and we made good use of it. Mama had a big table where she was able to prepare her homemade pizzas, calzones, and pasta fagioli. In the summertime, this became the perfect place for our frequent, extended family gatherings, which spread outside into the backyard through the basement door.

Our new neighbors were mostly Irish and German middle class residents. It would be quite some time before we could be accepted as equal neighbors. Mama planted a small garden for vegetables like the one we had in Ohio, and planted a flower bed where she could grow her beloved roses. She spent hours at her sewing machine making curtains, tablecloths, and dresses for my younger sisters. She made jam from the wild berries we picked in the woods near our home. I watched many times as she boiled tomatoes and bottled her special tomato sauce. Our oven saw plenty of use as she baked large loaves of bread and her specialty pizzas. Eventually, it was the pizzas that won over our neighbors. Fridays were usually pizza nights, since Catholics at that time did not eat meat on Fridays. She would always make sure to send a few over to our closest neighbors. They became more friendly each day. Whatever age the neighborhood children were, we had one to match. Our home became a gathering place for fun and games. For now, Mama was happy, cooking and decorating the house, and doing the many things she had, for a while, been deprived of doing.

But then there were also hard times. We thrive on the good memories, the others we try to suppress. My mother was trying her best to keep up with the neighborhood. Our house was pretty well furnished and by all appearances we were living a normal life. But that wasn't always the case. We have since lived such a blessed and joyful life, I am reluctant to recount those few years with their less pleasant memories, however they are not easily forgotten. Owning a home meant having expenses we hadn't had before. Each month Mama had less money to meet the household needs. Some everyday necessities had now become a luxury. I had no toothbrush or toothpaste. I learned to clean my teeth with a washcloth and baking soda. I never owned pajamas and slept in my underwear. I began wearing hand-me-down clothing from my three older brothers. By the time they got to me they were well worn. I became used to wearing shoes with holes in them and learned to line them with cardboard so I would not get holes in my stockings. When the toes of my socks wore through I would just fold them over. I did not complain to my mother because I knew there was not much she could do about it and I did not want to contribute to Mama's frustrations. There were no fancy meals. There were times when we skipped meals all together. I learned to eat pasta two or three nights a week because it was the most economical meal to make. The big meal was only on Sundays, meatballs, sausage, vegetables, Mama's special chicken soup, fruit and homemade pastries. I do not wish to dwell on this period of time because it was brief. These are not easy things to talk about now but they should be remembered. The good fortunes and happy times we enjoyed for so many years to come did not occur without sacrifices.

My younger sisters were spared some of the hardships we older siblings endured at the time. Using her skills at the sewing machine, Mama took great pains to keep her little girls well dressed. They weren't deprived of having little baby dolls and baby toys, and for the most part were unaware of the dire straits we were in. I think it was during those few years I became a "mama's boy." She had begun taking dressmaking jobs at home and was then hired by a theater company to make costumes. I watched her sit at her sewing machine for hours sewing costumes. She also took a job addressing envelopes for an advertising company. She addressed hundreds of envelopes every evening for a few dollars. As soon as I came home from school I would help her. It was very tedious work and I felt sorry she had to do this at the end of a long day. When my father left for work in the morning he would leave a few dollars on the kitchen table for her daily expenses. Though she couldn't afford to prepare the meals she would have liked, she always tried to make the meals appetizing with her special skills. By making her own dough she could make pasta in all different shapes so it wasn't like eating just spaghetti too often.

There was a door-to-door salesman who used to sell mostly dry goods and household products for time payments of a few dollars a week. My mother would use him whenever she was short on money. Occasionally, she couldn't meet the weekly payments and when he came to collect I would tell him my mother wasn't home. It would always make me nervous to lie to him and I don't think he always believed me. Then I began to see just how serious the situation was. My mother would get violent headaches every now and then. We soon found out whenever she got too far behind in the payment of a bill the worry would bring on an episode. My concern for her health caused me to forget any feelings I had about what I might be missing in life. It also became so noticeable that my father, who was not prone to showing his emotions very often, was also becoming worried about her health. I suspect he began having second thoughts about the choices he had made over the years. Right or wrong, good or bad, the decisions they made could be justified by the complete faith and love they had for one another. The struggle lasted only a couple of years. Then my father's business began doing well. Albert and Raymond were both working and Mama supplemented the family income with the few dollars she was earning. The future began to look brighter.

At that time, an event occurred which I have never been able to explain. Mama and I were home alone, she was cooking and I was building a model airplane. Suddenly we heard a loud crash coming from the basement. Mama came and held my hand for a few minutes visibly shaken. Still holding hands we went into the basement. There was nothing visible that could possibly have caused that noise. A few hours later Mama received a telegram from Ohio with the information that my father's mother had passed away. We never learned the source of that event. Neither of us ever told anyone what had happened.

Meanwhile, other families from Valsinni who had settled in New Jersey were also growing. They kept in touch with each other, sometimes giving help when needed. My mother and father, and a few close friends, decided to organize a society of the people from their hometown in Italy. They named it the Valsinnese Society, with the patron saint of Valsinni, San Fabiano, as their patron saint. They celebrated Mass together annually followed by a bountiful dinner. Groups of them would become regular visitors to our home on Sundays. They would bring their musical instruments and my mother would supply the food, usually pizzas, as they enjoyed my father's homemade wine and played their favorite Italian songs well into the evening, and their children would enjoy the luxury of playing in the woods with my siblings and me. They began doing each other the honor of becoming godparents of each other's children, sponsoring them at Confirmation, and hopefully arranging a few marriages. Those were unforgettable times that we would cherish forever.

Family entertainment at home
Papa Frank with Rose, Frances, Dolores, Eugene
Anthony, Raymond & Albert

(front) Frances, Rose
(rear) Eugene, Dolores, Anthony

Dolores & Eugene

Albert & Mama

Papa Frank's 58th birthday
Siblings left to right: Frances, Rose, Rita, Adeline, Albert, Raymond, Anthony, Eugene
Not pictured, Dolores

My Siblings

Sister Adeline
July 9, 1915 - September 27, 2013

Adeline was born in Niles, Ohio. For the first two years she was the pride and joy of the Fagnano family. After the birth of two more children, she became Mama's "little helper" babysitting and doing numerous household chores. Any free time she had she devoted to her studies. She was an honor student. A friend of the family had taken an interest in her talents and offered her free piano lessons. With her usual perseverance, she became an accomplished pianist, a talent she enjoyed for the rest of her life. As a young girl, she often accompanied our violinist father and clarinetist brother at family gatherings and celebrations. When she was sixteen years old, Adeline was called on to make a big sacrifice, she had to leave school in Niles and accompany our father to New Jersey where he'd hoped to find work once again as a barber. Heartbroken because she was in line to become Valedictorian of her graduating class, she reluctantly joined our father. She began working as a seamstress in a dress shop and in no time was promoted to forelady. She was able to attend night school to earn her diploma. The rest of our ever-growing family then settled in New Jersey. Being the oldest of nine children, Adeline helped our mother with raising the younger children. A young man, Dan Verina, who was also from Niles and settled in New Jersey, had become friends with our father and was often a visitor at our home. He and Adeline began dating and eventually married. They lived in several apartments before buying their home on Park Avenue in Fairview, a few short blocks from our home on North 8th Street. Dan was an auto mechanic and he rented space in a large garage and eventually owned his own repair shop. My sister handled all the bookkeeping for his business, skills she had mastered in night school. At the same time, the next generation of the Fagnano family began with the birth of their daughter, Daniella, followed by their twins, Cynthia and Michael. Adeline was a devoted parishioner of Our Lady Of Grace Catholic Church in Fairview, and became active in the local Parent Teacher Association, serving many years as president. She also chaired a chapter of the American Heart Association, her favorite charity. Because of her popularity she was often sought after by local politicians for her support. (I can attribute much of the success in my four terms as a borough councilman to her influence.) In the 1960's, she and her husband Dan purchased property in the Catskill Mountains in the town of Margaretville, New York. Over the years, they converted the tiny four-room cabin into a beautiful mountain home which they offered to any of us to use as a vacation spot. Later in life Adeline taught Kindergarten for many years at Epiphany Catholic School in Cliffside Park, and then became the music teacher at Our Lady of Grace Catholic School. She held that position until her retirement, when she was no longer physically able to continue. She never lost her love of music and she continued to play the piano until she passed away at the age of ninety-eight.

Adeline at her piano, Fairview NJ

Dan & Adeline

Brother Albert
November 9, 1917 - July 19, 2002

Albert was born in Niles, Ohio, the second child in the family. At the age of fifteen, Albert had to leave Niles in order to join our father and our sister, Adeline, who had already moved to New Jersey in search of a better life for our family. He and Adeline worked together at the dress shop until the rest of the family arrived. After living in several apartments, our family finally moved into our own home, and Albert began working at a local produce store. He was a very hard worker and learned his trade well. It would eventually become his lifelong career, a far cry from his earlier days at the "sweatshop." Albert possessed a humble and gracious personality throughout his life. His black, wavy hair and green eyes complimented his beautiful smile. Because of his skill as a ballroom dancer he was often sought after by young ladies as a partner for the jitterbug contests in which he won many trophies. He was a talented musician, playing saxophone and clarinet in big bands and combos. He always had a love for horses. He owned a complete riding outfit: boots, jodhpurs and a fancy shirt. (I made good use of his outfit when I finally grew into it.) He often took his dates riding at the local stables. Albert was finally enjoying the pleasures of life that were denied him for so long. And then World War II broke out. The few years of tranquility he had enjoyed so well were over. He enlisted in the cavalry and began training at Fort Knox, Kentucky. While there, an event occurred that would eventually help him cope with the inevitable horrors of war. On a weekend pass at a chaperoned dance at the local USO, he met a young girl, Marjorie Redd. She was not only beautiful, but a very good dancer. They were instantly attracted to each other and met again a number of times before he was sent overseas. Unfortunately, the horse cavalry had disbanded and became mechanized. He wound up in an Armored Division under General George Patton and was sent to France where he served until the end of the war. Albert and Marjorie carried on their courtship by mail for the next four years. At war's end Albert returned to a different world back home. He went back to work, and headed to Kentucky where he and Marjorie married. He brought her home to Fairview, and they repeated the ceremony for the family there. After attending barber school, Albert worked for a short time with Papa, but without enough business to sustain two salaries he decided to return to his old occupation with the A&P company where he remained until his retirement.

  Housing was scarce, so Albert and Marjorie lived at our family home for two years until they were able to find an apartment in the next town. Later on, my wife and I were able to rent an apartment in the same building. There they welcomed their first son, Mark. A few years later, Albert and Margie were able to purchase a home in Fairview on Park Avenue, across the street from our sister, Adeline. That same year, I bought a house up the street next to our brother, Anthony. Albert and Margie welcomed another son, Frank, a few years later. Albert's dream was to someday own a small nightclub where he and his brothers would work and even provide the music together. That dream was never realized, but Margie and Albert had each other and they both had the love and companionship of the family. They grew old together, until Margie, after a short illness passed away. His love of music, and dedication to caring for his sons and grandchildren sustained him until he died at the age of eighty-four. I spent my last evening with him by his bedside, listening to a tape of us playing during one of our jam sessions.

He passed away the next morning.

Mama Rose & Albert

Albert and his saxophone

Albert & Margie

Brother Raymond
January 12, 1921 - May 21, 2008

Raymond was the third child in our family. He and brother Albert, lived the same childhood until Albert had to move to New Jersey. He remained in high school until his senior year when he chose to drop out. He did learn to play the trumpet while in high school and was a member of the high school band. He enjoyed music but was never really as interested in it as Adeline and Albert. Raymond was always somewhat of a renegade in the family. He had already shown signs of restlessness and a desire to seek future adventures. After leaving school he began working at the same produce store as Albert, delivering orders. One day, while out on a delivery to a wealthy family in town, Raymond met a pretty girl named Caroline. There was a brief mutual attraction that was put on hold when our family bought a home in the nearby town of Fairview. Raymond then began working at a local A&P Supermarket. By chance he and Caroline would once again meet when our sister, Rita, entered the same high school as Caroline. Rita and Caroline became close friends, and Caroline became a frequent visitor at our home. That gave her and Raymond a chance to see each other and renew their friendship. They became very fond of each other, but they had to keep their relationship a secret from her family. She was a talented pianist and taught Raymond how to play the piano. Although he enjoyed playing the trumpet, he gave that up and became more interested in the piano. (I took his old trumpet when I was about ten years old and learned to play by ear, not knowing how to read music.) Raymond became an extremely talented pianist and played professionally for many years. He was also skilled as a craftsman, artist, and mechanic. Everyone enjoyed the antics of our brother, Raymond. He masked his emotions with his sense of humor. While working at the A & P he met a local girl who was also attending the same high school as Rita and Caroline. She was a beautiful Irish girl named Margaret Shea. There were no restraints on their relationship, so they were free to court with no restrictions. He was torn between two loves, but he finally decided to spend the rest of his life with his new love, Margaret. Raymond joined the Air Force during World War II and was stationed in Arizona. While still in the service he came home on leave and he and Margaret were married. They spent the early years of marriage living with Margaret's mother. They had three children, Patricia, Donna, and Raymond. A few years later they bought a beautiful home on a large piece of property in Rivervale, New Jersey, about eighteen miles from Fairview. Margie's widowed mother and an uncle came to live with them. It would be many years before Raymond and his wife would have their home all to themselves.

I suspect he chose that town because of its proximity to a nearby airfield which was used by the civil air patrol after the war. He spent as much time as he could at that airfield, occasionally taking a flight with the older pilots. Within a few years, however, the airfield was abandoned. In time, his children and grandchildren would share his fascination with airplanes and his love of flying. Some even became pilots.

Raymond worked his way up to being an A & P manager, and then decided to venture into something different. He became employed in the automobile industry where he soon acquired an executive position. He often entertained employees at company parties with his talent of playing the piano. Anywhere there was a piano, brother Raymond could be found, he had an insatiable love for playing. Everyone's house had a piano and whenever he and Margie would drive down to Park Avenue there would always be a jam session.

We were somewhat disappointed, but not so much surprised, that Raymond had decided to move such a distance away from where the rest of us had already settled. Raymond had an independent personality and liked to follow his own path. Happily, before long, Raymond and Margie's home, though a distance away, became the site of many Sunday afternoon family gatherings, especially since they had a swimming pool. The basement was converted into a music room where we enjoyed many brotherly jam sessions, with our brother Anthony (who did not play an instrument) sitting in the rocking chair, beer in hand, enjoying the music. As time went by we would still get together regularly to play there. Eventually, Albert could not make the trip and when he passed away it left Raymond and I to carry on without him. We continued to play our music together whenever we could until Raymond suffered a stroke and passed away at the age of eighty-seven. It seemed to me as though the clock was beginning to tick too fast and my world was changing with it.

Raymond's handbuilt airplane

Raymond at the piano

Ray & Marge

Sister Rita
August 8, 1923 - November 30, 2008

    My sister, Rita, the fourth of my siblings, was born after our family moved to New Jersey the first time. She was a good student and the first in our family to graduate high school. All through her teenage years Rita was Mama's biggest helper. She spent most of her time doing housework and homework, with little time for social activities. Because she was so pretty Mama kept a watchful eye on her. While attending high school she became acquainted with Raymond's teenage girlfriend, Caroline, and also with his future wife, Margaret. After graduation, Rita became employed in a defense plant making radio parts for the war industry. It was then that Tom Bruno, a friend of ours from Ohio who visited our home frequently, announced he was getting married. He was a tailor by trade and he had met his future wife, Mary Campagna, at work. She was a widow with four children. During their many visits, their son, Gene, a war veteran, became attracted to Rita. This made Mama and Papa very happy. He was Italian, Catholic, and the son of a good friend. After a brief courtship, Rita and Gene were married and moved to Gene's family home in Brooklyn, New York. Sharing a home with his mother and three sisters became difficult, especially after the birth of their son, Nicholas. Much to Rita's relief, Gene agreed to move back to Fairview, New Jersey. They rented several apartments before buying a home in a neighboring town. Rita was happy to be back in the family circle. She worked days and attended night school to become a teacher. Gene was employed as an engineer at the Nabisco Company. Rita made a career for herself teaching elementary school first at St. John the Baptist School in Fairview and then at Epiphany School in Cliffside Park. Nicholas completed a PhD and moved to Wisconsin where he married and had two children. Years after their retirement, Rita and Gene made the heartfelt decision to move to Wisconsin, to be with Nicholas, his wife and their two grandchildren. After both their grandchildren finished their education and left home Rita and Gene were anxious to move back home to Jersey, They began making plans but it was not to be. Unfortunately, Rita passed away in her sleep at the age of eighty-five, and Gene died a few years after.

Rita & Gene

Albert, Rita, & Raymond

Brother Anthony
August 21, 1926 - January 3, 2000

Anthony, the fifth child, was the "Macho Man" of the family. Because we were only two years apart, we lived basically the same childhood. His legendary antics began at a very early age, he was always a little on the mischievous side. One day, when we were youngsters, my brother decided to play barber with me. I was only three years old at the time and had a beautiful head of hair. With a pair of Papa's barber scissors, Anthony proceeded to give me my first haircut. Afterwards, afraid of the inevitable consequences, my brother hid under the front porch the rest of the day. Only the humor of the situation saved him. As teenagers, Anthony and I worked in a bowling alley for a time setting up the pins. During the summers, he began working on a delivery truck delivering ice. In his teen years, Anthony had his share of mischief, often causing my mother unnecessary concern. He liked working at a local pool hall setting up the tables where he could earn money to buy cigarettes. The truant officer was a constant visitor at our home and a forbidden swim in the Hudson River usually got him a tongue-lashing. He didn't care for school and dropped out in his Junior Year. He then began working full-time in a factory that produced tobacco pipes. He was very free-spirited and the most athletic of the brothers. He was well-muscled and very adept at all sports. He could bowl, swim, dive, dance, roller skate and even enjoyed gymnastics. As he grew older he outgrew his juvenile antics and began to mature. He had taken up roller skating as a hobby and uncharacteristically became very talented at it. His masculine appearance and easy going ways increased his popularity with the girls. It was difficult to picture him dancing with the girls on roller skates. He enjoyed the physical aspects of skating but had no interest in any of his female partners.

Anthony was eager to join our brothers in the service, but with two sons already serving, our father would not give him permission until he was eighteen. He joined the Navy and served his time on a destroyer in the South Pacific theater of World War II. He then returned home to enjoy the family he left behind. He had matured during his years in the Navy and began to think about plans for the future. Harriet Gratta, a friend of our sister, Rita, had always been a frequent visitor to our home, but now Anthony was beginning to notice she had grown up into a beautiful young lady. Much to everyone's surprise they began dating and "Macho Man" eventually married her. He attended school under the GI Bill and with the tutelage of our brother-in-law, Dan Verina, Anthony became a skilled mechanic and joined him in his auto shop. After living with Harriet's parents a short while, they moved into an apartment on Park Avenue in Fairview next to our sister, Adeline, and a few years later purchased a house on the same block. They had two children, James and Kathy.

With his skills as a craftsman, Anthony designed their home to become a gathering place for old and young alike. Many backyard picnics, holidays and family celebrations were held there. With his sense of humor and flamboyant ways, he would be the center of many incidents throughout the years. Not having had any grandchildren of their own, Harriet and Anthony were devoted to their many nieces and nephews. The many years of happy times together ended with the passing of his beloved wife. From then on he was not the same. I tried to get him interested in hobbies, raising tropical fish, making lawn ornaments and building model airplanes. He found it very difficult to deal with his loss. Not long afterwards, he was hospitalized with a case of "twenty-four hour flu". His condition deteriorated and at the age of seventy-three, with his brothers by his side, the Macho Man passed away. The loss of the first of the four brothers had a sobering effect on the surviving brothers.

Albert & Anthony

Anthony & Harriet

Anthony

Harriet & Anthony

Sister Dolores
March 30, 1930

    Dolores, born in Niles, Ohio, was the seventh child and two years younger than me. Papa was very happy to welcome another girl after having two more boys, and Mama raised her new daughter with vigor. Dolores was a baby when we moved from Niles to New Jersey. After we'd finally moved into our home on North 8th Street in Fairview she was able to enjoy a typical childhood. She was a happy-go-lucky child and everything was a game to her. She loved playing with her dolls and carriages and often tagged along after me. (In later years, this memory prompted her to send me a poem she'd written, "The Bestist.") As she grew older, Dolores became somewhat of a tomboy, playing in the woods near our house, especially climbing trees, where she'd wait for our brother, Albert, to arrive home from work. Dolores was a bright student while attending parochial school, participating in many activities, and making many new friends. During her early school years she entertained the idea of becoming a nun, which, surprisingly, upset Mama at the time. Dolores graduated with honors in 1948, and was awarded a scholarship to nursing school, which she was not able to accept. Papa had experienced his first heart attack, so she chose to take a job at the Metropolitan Insurance Company in New York where she worked for four years in the medical division, helping to support our parents. At that time, a friend of hers asked if she would be interested in a blind date. Her neighbor's son was bringing home two Navy buddies from Norfolk, Virginia, for the weekend, and Joseph Deery, a handsome Irish sailor from Pennsylvania was chosen to be her date on July 29, 1950. It was love at first sight. After six months of dating on weekend leaves, Dolores and Joe became engaged. He was sent overseas to Africa, assigned to the Navy Air Corp as a radar technician on a reconnaissance plane during the Korean Conflict. After he returned, they spent time securing their relationship and planning for the future. Joe lived in Pennsylvania and our two families knew little about each other, but this proved to be no obstacle to their upcoming wedding plans. They were married in 1952. Unable to find an apartment in New Jersey, they settled into an apartment in Drexel, Pennsylvania. Joe worked for a time at Piasecki Helicopter, and then moved on to a career with the Bell Telephone Company. While happily settling into married life, Dolores began to miss her family in New Jersey, with communication being limited to phone calls and occasional visits. She became more lonely and depressed, prompting our mother to take quick train trips to visit her. Then our father passed away the month before the birth of Dolores and Joe's first child, Jeanne, in 1953. After the birth of their second child, Karen, they moved into a new community developed for veterans in Levittown. With good schools, churches, swimming pools, and friendly neighbors, it was a perfect place to raise a family. Theirs continued to grow with the birth of their daughter, Gail, and son, Joseph. They began to live with vigor. They made many new friends, and were enjoying the sense of a community that became like family. They took on the Heart Fund Drive in memory of our Papa. As their children grew, Dolores was able to help out financially by teaching remedial reading for the Bucks County

Remedial Unit, assigned to her parish school. She became a church lector, eucharistic minister and went to Philadelphia once a week to the St. Charles Seminary for the Diaconate Program.

Dolores and Joe devoted all their time and energy to providing their children with a college education. With their family thriving, they settled down to enjoy the fruits of their labor. Much to their delight they were blessed with many grandchildren and great-grandchildren. And then sadness came when Dolores watched her husband suddenly become ill. After a long, brave struggle to survive, he was gone. Dolores had survived many losses and disappointments in her life before but this was a devastating blow. Her family gathered around her and did their best to console her. Surrounded by these loved ones, Dolores realized the blessings Joe had worked so hard for and had left to her, and she would be able to continue her life as they had planned. She became interested in learning how to play the piano and violin. She is an amateur artist and very talented at needlepoint. She also enjoys writing poetry and songs. As a devoted wife and mother her only concern was keeping her family together. She often thinks of the family events in Fairview that she had missed while raising her family, but as I reminded her, she was also spared being there during the sad times, witnessing the loss of loved ones. In Fairview we were reminded of our loved ones every day, their empty homes, their children and their friends.

Dolores continues to devote her life to helping and caring for others. I have been the beneficiary of her efforts numerous times. She remains a role model for her children, with determination and unending love. She continues the journey that began so many years ago with her one and only love. As "their song" says, "....they were not too young at all."

Dolores

Joe & Dolores

Dolores & Joe

Sister Rose
February 28, 1933

Rose was born in North Bergen, New Jersey, the eighth child in our family. She was a beautiful baby, with fair skin, blond hair and blue eyes, unusual features for a typical Italian descended from our region in Italy. She was an infant when our family moved from apartment to apartment and was four years old when we moved to Fairview. Rosie was an excellent student, breezed through grammar school, always eager to learn as much as possible. When she entered high school she began to show the characteristics that would define her later on in life. She made friends easily and became involved in every project possible. She joined choirs in high school and church, learned to read music, and learned to play the piano and organ. After high school she became involved in church affairs, working as the church secretary for a while. Never satisfied with being just a participant, she was always at the forefront of her many ventures and she accepted any new assignment as a challenge. After our father suffered a fatal heart attack in 1953, Rosie was left as the sole support of Mama at home. Albert and Margie, my wife and I had found apartments, and our youngest sister, Frances, married and moved into an apartment. Rosie proved to be well capable of handling the daunting task of caring for a grieving mother, to whom she was devoted. Then a ray of sunshine poked through what had been a somewhat cloudy sky.

A life-long friend of our father, Hubert Stigliano, a fellow Valsinnese, and his wife, Philomena, were very dear friends, and frequent visitors to our home with their four sons. As teenagers, we all enjoyed playing with one another as our parents partied and reminisced. One of their sons, Bert, was a mild mannered, reserved young man, a real gentleman, well liked by all who met him. Growing up together, he always felt like one of the family. He and I were about the same age, and he also served a tour in the Army. Eventually, he and Rosie began to enjoy each other's company, much to the delight of both families. Mama's future was not going to be an obstacle to their wedding plans. As testimony to Bert's genuine character, he readily agreed to live with and help support our mother after he and Rosie were married. Papa's absence at their wedding was most felt by our Mama. Two years later, Rosie and Bert welcomed the birth of their son, Robert. Bert had become a TV repairman and opened up a small business. They continued to look after Mama, making life for her as pleasant as possible. And Mama enjoyed caring for baby Robert. After he started school, Rosie volunteered as the church secretary, and then worked as a secretary at a public school. Mama was offered a job as cook for the priests at our church rectory, a position she thoroughly enjoyed. She was free to cook the meals she was most capable of. These were happy times for Mama. She now had a little extra income and time to spend with her growing family.

Rosie's varied fields of interest were all met with the same enthusiasm. Active in church, charity, and political affairs, she was soon recognized as an outstanding personality in our town of Fairview, an asset which proved beneficial in the election of her husband to the Board Of Education. Rosie was a committee chairperson in her district and became involved in all local elections, (including my four terms as councilman.) She was the first woman to be elected president of the Lions Club. A deeply religious conviction enabled her to deal with her own personal problems while giving comfort to others in need. She had eventually gone to work for Commonwealth Trust Bank, and then Midlantic Bank from which she retired thirty years later as an assistant manager.

When Bert's father passed away in 1986, he and Rosie moved in with his mother in Fort Lee, New Jersey, where they lived until Mrs. Stigliano moved into an assisted living home. Rosie and Bert finally bought a home of their own quite a distance from our hometown of Fairview, in Rockland County, NY. Sadly, their enjoyment together there was brief, lasting only one year when Bert became seriously ill and passed away. Rosie had no choice but to sell this home, and move back closer to her son, Robert, and his family. She continued her work with the Lions Club, stayed active for a while with the church choir back in Fairview, and then became active in her local church, using her banking experience to assist with their financial operations. A very devout person, she relies on a deep faith in God to help all those for whom she prays. She stands ready and willing to accept any challenge, has a fierce loyalty and respect for family matters, and limits all her memories to pleasant ones. A sister, mother, grandmother and friend....she will always be an achiever.

Bert & Rosie

Rosie

Sister Frances
November 27, 1934 - October 2, 2018

    The birth of our sister, Frances, the ninth and final child in our family, came about under unusual circumstances. It was Thanksgiving Day, and we were all enjoying the festivities in our apartment. I was only six years old and didn't fully comprehend the event taking place at the time. Our mother, with the help of a midwife, was in her bedroom giving birth to our new sister. So we ended up having much more to celebrate that day than Thanksgiving. Frances was a beautiful baby and she would maintain that beauty throughout her life, and as the baby of the family she would always be referred to as, "Little Frances." As a teenager she was much more adventurous than her older sisters. She possessed a beautiful voice and could always be coerced into singing at family gatherings. During and after her high school years her demure personality brought her many friends, male and female. Being the youngest and the last of the children, she was afforded much more freedom than her sisters were allowed before her. This was beginning to become a concern for Mama. Carefree and fun-loving, she was the center of attraction among her many friends. One of them was a young man named William Terrazzi. His good looks and charm won him favor over his many rivals, and he and Frances were soon keeping steady company. Before their romance could go any further, Bill had to serve his term in the Army. They became engaged, but then our father suffered his fatal heart attack. Bill finished his tour and upon his discharge he and Frances were married. Their wedding ceremony was dampened by the loss of our Papa as all concern was turned to our Mama. Bill began working as a truck driver, and he and Frances lived for a short time with Mama before moving into a nearby apartment. The birth of their daughter, Theresa, was a happy occasion. She was later joined by another daughter, Dawn. Eventually, they were able to purchase a home in nearby Rutherford, New Jersey. Eager to raise a large family, three more children were welcomed into their family, Renee, William, and John.

During the years that followed there were many good times and some troubled ones. They were mostly a happy couple enjoying life and living a dream for many years. Frances worked for a while at a bakery and in a school cafeteria. She and Bill tried to maintain a close relationship with our extended family. Unfortunately, Frances began suffering bouts of depression. As time went on, Frances sought medical solutions for her troubled mind. And, her marriage was dissolving, which was also causing her to suffer. It finally came to be that after their children were grown, she and Bill were divorced. They sold their house, and Frances moved into an apartment. She was happy for a while and her life was pretty much normal again. She regained the personality she had enjoyed for so many years. Still an attractive lady, she was able to acquire a few new relationships. The family made attempts to guide her and encourage her to change the lifestyle she was leading. Her situation finally came to an end after one last attempt at a new relationship resulted in a separation. And then, tragically, cancer claimed the life of their beautiful daughter Dawn.

Unable to live with any of her children, Frances took one last opportunity to settle down. She entered a senior citizens apartment in southern New Jersey and finally returned to living a normal life. Being younger than most of the residents there, she became very popular. She entertained the other residents by singing and playing the piano. Soon she had made many new friends. She met one gentleman, Steven Barnes, with whom she would become a close friend. They eventually married and continued to live in the home together. Steve was a loving husband and they were very happy. Frances was finally enjoying life once again, although she gradually lost touch with the rest of the family. She lived quite a distance away, but we were all comforted in knowing she was well and happy. And then her health began to fail, her years of heartaches and struggles finally took their toll. After a short illness, she passed away at the age of eighty-three.

Me with Frances

The Fagnano Sisters - (back row) Adeline, Rita, Dolores, (front) Francis, Rosie

All the ladies. Seated, left to right: Dolores, Rosie, Frances
Standing, left to right: Edna (Koludrovich), Rita, Harriet (Gratta), Margie (Shea), Margie (Redd), Adeline

Husbands and Wives

Standing: Harriet Gratta (Anthony), Bert Stigliano (Rose), Edna Koludrovich (Eugene), Margie Shea (Raymond), Gene Campagna (Rita), Margie Redd (Albert).
Kneeling: Bill Terrazzi (Frances), Joe Deery (Dolores), Dan Verina (Adeline)

Frances, Rosie, Dolores, Eugene, Anthony, Rita, Raymond, Albert, Adeline

    To have given a detailed biography of each of my brothers and sisters would be more of a task than I could handle. But for the benefit of my children and grandchildren, I will use this opportunity to elaborate on my own personal biography.

Eugene
January 18, 1928

As the oldest surviving member of the nine Fagnano children, I feel privileged to share my memories of the small role I played in the legacy of our family and our journey through time.

I was born in Niles, Ohio. When I was three years old Mama and Papa moved us to New Jersey. At the time, we were a family of seven siblings, four brothers and three sisters. We would later welcome two more girls. One of my earliest memories from my childhood is of an unfortunate accident I had. One day, while playing with my brother, Anthony, I was unintentionally the cause of some unnecessary grief for my mother. There was a steep driveway next to our apartment and Anthony and I were riding down it with our kiddie cars. Instead of turning onto the sidewalk at the bottom of the driveway, I rolled right out into the street. I was struck by a car that had very little time to stop. Fortunately, I was not seriously hurt, but just to make sure, the driver brought my mother and I to a local doctor's office. He said all I had suffered were some large bruises. My mother insisted on bringing me to see my father and assure him I was not seriously hurt. The shaken driver of the car gave my mother twenty-five dollars as a token settlement and I was treated to an ice cream cone. Years later, at one of our family gatherings, my mother was telling the story of my accident and she remarked that twenty-five dollars was a lot of money in those days, and that she had paid the rent with it that month. In an attempt to be funny, I said, "Yeah, after that, every time the rent was due I had to hide the kiddie car." My mother didn't appreciate the humor in my remark and I regretted saying it.

We spent the next few years moving to several apartments. the last one being the one next to the Jewish synagogue and the local firehouse. From that last apartment we moved to our home in Fairview where, at the age of seven, I began a whole new life. Playing in the woods surrounding our home was a whole new experience. I soon had many new friends. There was a small clearing in the woods where we would gather to roast potatoes on a small fire. We made it our special meeting place. I grew up playing the usual games - stickball, basketball, and sometimes a game of touch football.

A memory that still lingers in my mind took place on my eighth birthday. My mother baked a cake for the occasion and told me I could invite a few friends to our house for a party. This was a real treat for me. Before that, birthdays had often come and gone unnoticed during the hard times. There was an Irish family living a few houses away from ours. The owner was an elected official in town, and had four daughters and one son. One of the daughters, Maureen, was my age, very pretty and friendly, and I had a secret crush on her. Her family was considered to be upper middle class. I thought there was little chance she would say yes, but I invited her to my party anyway. I was shocked when she said yes. We definitely lived on "opposite sides of the tracks" and I wasn't sure if she would be allowed to attend. She brought me a present, a beautiful leather aviator's hat with plastic goggles. I cherished that present and I began to think maybe it meant she liked me a little bit. Although we never shared another moment again, I spent the rest of my childhood fantasizing over her. I named my ship models after her, carved her initials in a tree, wrote poems about her and would walk past her house whenever she was outside just so I could say hello and see her smile. I spent the rest of my youth with the local boys playing ball and other street games. We attended different schools and had different friends. Our conversations were limited to casual greetings whenever we saw each other. In my early teens, during more ambitious moments, I even wrote love letters to her. I never received any in return, nor did I expect any. My only purpose was to let her know how I felt. I did make one feeble attempt to date her, inviting her to attend a movie with me, which she graciously declined. I never took the liberty of asking her again. This exciting time of fantasizing about a secret love was futile and soon passed. I made new friends and had new interests during my high school years, although occasionally, Maureen would still be in my thoughts. As I grew older I realized this whole experience was a real case of puppy love. We each got married and went our separate ways, our paths not crossing again until many years later.

By the time I reached the sixth grade in school I began to get involved in different activities. I was appointed as a school crossing guard, we were called "patrol boys" and I was assigned to a corner near the school to see that the children crossed safely. I was very proud of my badge and the white belt that I wore. Soon after, when a drum and bugle corps was formed, I learned to play the bugle and for several years marched in the parades. Years later it led to me learning to play the trumpet and I became a musician.

A historic Event occurred that would change our lives forever, the bombing of Pearl Harbor on December 7, 1941. America's participation in World War II had begun. At the age of fifteen I became an air raid warden. I received a flashlight, whistle and a white helmet and during the blackout I would patrol the streets warning people to turn off all their lights. At that time I was the youngest warden. It afforded me a little taste of responsibility. I began building WWII models of war planes. I became very interested in aeronautics. In a strange turn of events the high school was offering a class in aeronautics due to the war. The teacher that was assigned to teach the course was totally unprepared for it. He confided in me after class one day that he was having great difficulty explaining the new course. Being aware of my knowledge of aircraft recognition he actually asked me if I would assist him during the class. I was very flattered and honored to do so. It was one of the few things I enjoyed during my years of high school.

My brother, Albert, was the first to join the Army and was soon sent to France. My brother, Raymond, because of his love of flying, enlisted in the Air Force. My brother, Anthony, had to wait until he was eighteen years old to join the Navy. I was still in high school, not yet old enough to join my brothers. Suddenly our home felt empty. My sister, Adeline, was now married and had her own home. Eventually, three brothers were on active duty, followed by me in the post war draft. It was customary during the war to put a flag in your window with a star if you had someone serving in the military. At the war's end our flag had four stars, the only one in our town with four stars. Feeling the way I missed my brothers during the war, I can only imagine what my mother and father felt. I watched them both turn gray during those four years. My mother would wait for the mailman every day. Whenever she received a letter from one of her sons he would ring the bell and tell her. I watched her writing letters every night, often with tears in her eyes. It would make me cry. My father was always a very patriotic man, and he would ask me to decorate his barbershop with patriotic items. I made model military airplanes and hung them in the window with American flags and pictures of soldiers. He had very little schooling but kept a little notepad which he would use to practice writing. Although it could take days to write one letter he managed to write to my brother, Albert, who was overseas. At home, we were living under wartime restrictions. Many things were being rationed, sugar, gasoline, cigarettes, even silk and rubber tires. Everyone was working war time jobs. It seemed like everything happened so quickly. It felt strange not sharing a bedroom with my three brothers. However, after I enlisted in the Army to fulfill my obligation with the occupation forces there were plenty of men to share my sleeping quarters with. And for the first time in my life, I had a bed of my own.

With three brothers all serving in the armed forces it became necessary for me to find employment to help my father support our family. It would be a couple of years before I could join my brothers in military service. My years in high school were not very pleasant and I looked forward to graduating and getting on with my life. When I reached the age of sixteen I applied for my working papers and began looking for employment the next day. After having no success finding work, I stopped at a local White Castle and met a friend of mine working there. When I told him I had been looking for a job all day he advised me that his boss was looking to hire someone. He would be in the next morning to check the inventory and I could speak to him then. I met with him and after a brief interview he hired me.

Albert – from horses to tanks

Raymond, Crew Chief, B-25 Bomber

Anthony, Anchors aweigh

I was the last to go

The White Castle Years

I began working full-time after school at White Castle. During the summer I worked the day shift and it gave me the opportunity to enjoy somewhat of a social life. Going to school during the day and working full time after school kept me well occupied, so I began a new phase in my life. I felt a sense of pride when I could hand my mother a check every week to ease her problems a little bit. After all the hard times we had been through, my every thought was to please my mother. In my younger days I was afraid God would punish me if I ever did something wrong. Now my only thoughts were not to do anything that might ever hurt or disappoint my mother in any way. That fear kept me out of a lot of bad situations for years to come. My experiences while working at the White Castle would test those concerns to the limit. I was just sixteen years old when I began working there. While still in school I worked after school from four o'clock in the afternoon to ten o'clock at night. I had led a somewhat sheltered life up until then and soon began to learn the facts of life. A group of motorcycle riders made the White Castle their meeting place and taught me to drive a motorcycle. It was something I enjoyed very much along with horseback riding. On the night before entering the service I had a small farewell party. I had to bring my love home before nine o'clock as usual. My brother-in-law Dan loaned me his car to take her home. Much to my surprise, ten of the motorcycle friends came to bid me farewell. When I drove away to bring my love home they circled around my car and escorted me as if I was some kind of dignitary. I found it very amusing and was very grateful for the show of friendship.

Before the war, the White Castle hired only men. During the war years they were forced to also hire women. With everybody working in defense plants earning good salaries it was difficult finding employees to work at lesser jobs. My coworkers came mostly from the South. They had been mostly cotton pickers, making very little money while doing hard work. They were good workers and enjoyed living here. They worked hard but also loved to party. Some were married and others were just living together. This was shocking to me but I learned to accept it. It sometimes became uncomfortable for me and embarrassing because they liked to tease me about my innocence. They often invited me to their drinking parties but I always declined, dreading what my mother would think if she ever found out. On one particular occasion I was caught in an unavoidable situation which could have been a catastrophe for me. My coworkers had all been living in a boarding house together. My supervisor would come to the White Castle in the morning to check the inventory and collect the night's receipts. One morning he came in and found me working alone. He asked where the help was and I told him they hadn't yet turned up for work. He knew they must have been partying the night before and were probably sleeping late. He was very angry and told me to go to the boarding house where they were staying and tell them if they did not come to work immediately they would be fired. He said he would work the counter until I got back. It was a fifteen-minute ride by bus, and when I arrived at the boarding house I found them all still sleeping. I woke them and told them what the supervisor had said, then I hurried back to work. We waited patiently for over an hour, they still had not arrived. Then a police officer, whom I knew as a steady customer, came in and spoke to my supervisor. He told them the workers had been arrested for, "living in open lewdness." If my supervisor would go down to the police station and pay the fine, they would be let out of jail. Having no choice, my supervisor bailed them out with a warning. If they ever missed work again they would be fired. I was completely shaken by the whole experience. Had I been at that boarding house just a few minutes longer I would have been arrested with the others. It would have broken my mother's heart and I would have had a tough time explaining the whole event. My supervisor, who had become a father figure to me, warned me to not be influenced by my coworkers. I was able to ignore their teasing after that and it removed any temptations I might have had in the future.

    A more pleasant and somewhat amusing incident occurred when I became friendly with a young lady named Florence who worked in a dry cleaning store across the street from the White Castle. She was a very pretty girl and popular with the boys. We could see each other through the front windows of our workplaces and would wave to each other often during the day. Sometimes she would motion to me, indicating that she would like a hamburger. I would eagerly run across the street to oblige her. I felt privileged to be treated like a special friend of hers. One day, she beckoned me and I immediately responded. She invited me to sit in the back room with her while she ate the hamburger and had a container of milk. I felt honored because no one was ever allowed in the back room except employees. I was enjoying the moment when all of a sudden the warning bell on the front door sounded, indicating a customer was entering. Unfortunately, it was not a customer, it was her supervisor. She would come once a day to check the register, usually staying only five minutes or so, and would then go on to check the other stores. I saw her through the curtains in the doorway and became very frightened. My friend went out front to meet her. Fearing the supervisor might enter the back room, I took advantage of a pile of dirty clothes that was placed on the floor by laying down on the floor and covering myself with the dirty clothes. I laid there for four or five minutes, sweating and struggling to breathe, until the supervisor finally left. My friend looked shaken and I gave a sigh of relief. We looked at each other for a moment and then both of us began to laugh hysterically. I never went into the back room again.

One other memory, this one far more serious, comes to mind when I think back to my experiences while working at the Castle. I was working the night shift with two young ladies, and a little after midnight one of the ladies became sick. She complained of nausea and a violent headache. I advised her to go home and said we would cover for her. About an hour later the other girl said she, too, felt sick. I wasn't sure what to do, but when she began to feel worse I sent her home also. There were very few customers coming in at that time of night, but when one entered the diner he said he smelled gas. I didn't smell it so I served him and began checking the gas jets, finding nothing wrong. Then another customer came in and also said that he smelled gas. I served him and as soon as he left I locked the front door. I telephoned my supervisor, who lived about an hour away, and told him what was happening. He told me to keep the place shut down and he would come immediately. I did what he said, then went into the back room and laid down on a table to wait for him. The next thing I remember was his slapping my face and calling my name. He had carried me outside and I was sitting on the ground. He wanted to bring me to a hospital, but I insisted he just bring me home, which he did. I had been overcome by the gas and he got to me just in time. We found out later there was a break in a gas line out in the street, and the gas had traveled underground into the basement of the White Castle, filling it with fumes. My mother was never aware of this incident. She was happy I had a nice, clean job, wore a clean white shirt with a black bow tie, and could eat all I wanted.

Near the White Castle where I was working there was a taxi cab station and its owner was a steady customer. One day he asked me if I would be interested in driving a cab for him for a few hours a night. I said I would be glad to and started driving the following evening. One night after a few local calls, I received an urgent call from a lady saying she had to bring her baby to the doctor. When I arrived she was waiting for me, holding a baby blanket in her arms. I asked her for directions to the doctor's office and we drove away. Upon arriving at the office I noticed a sign on the front lawn that said "Veterinarian". It seems her baby was a pet cat.

A few nights later I received a call to drive a fare to Hoboken. I picked up three men whom I now believe may have been local bookies. They told me they had to catch a train in Hoboken and warned me I shouldn't be late. During the trip they kept urging me to drive faster. One of them became increasingly concerned about how fast I was driving but the other two just laughed at him. When I finally stopped at a red light he jumped out of the car and said, "You guys are crazy! I'll catch a bus." When I returned to the cab station the owner was waiting for me. He asked for my keys and told me I was fired. I was shocked and didn't know what to say. The gentleman who had jumped out of the car told him I was a reckless driver. I tried to explain to him that I was just following orders from the other two men but he didn't accept my excuse. My employment there only lasted a week and I never drove a cab again. After that I was content to go back to my job "slinging hamburgers".

Growing Up During Wartime

During the war, with all kinds of rationing going on, I was in a position to do favors for my customers in many different ways. Defense workers had become my steady customers. When a customer ordered a cup of coffee I would ask if they wanted sugar. If they said no, I would put a sugar cube aside in a jar. I saved the sugar for my steady customers who would often ask if I could spare some if they were celebrating a special occasion. I was happy to oblige them. When the vendor came to fill the cigarette machine he would have only a few cartons of name brands, the rest were all off-brands because the name brands were going overseas to the soldiers. I put aside some of the name brands for my steady customers. I gained some popularity because of this. I became acquainted with many bus drivers who came in for a fast cup of coffee in between runs, and I always served them quickly. I came to know many of them personally and rarely paid a fare when riding on one of their buses. The local police were also steady customers. While I worked the night shift it was comforting to know they were always nearby. One of my steady customers kindly loaned me his car for my prom night. It was a gesture I never forgot, and one of the many pleasant memories I have of working at the Castle.

One such pleasant memory is of the day a pretty, young high school girl from a neighboring town, whose name was Dolores, came into the diner during the summer school vacation. We struck up a pleasant conversation and I waited anxiously for her next visit to further our friendship. It came soon after and I invited her to go horseback riding with me. A few more dates followed, horseback riding and trips to the local ice cream parlor. Our meetings were only from the White Castle diner because she wouldn't tell me where she lived. After a few dates I decided to try and find out where she lived. She always boarded a bus near the diner to take her to the next town near her residence. One evening, after she left the ice cream parlor to go home, I got on my bicycle and decided to follow the bus. It was slow-moving and I had no trouble keeping up. She lived somewhere near the bottom of a very steep hill. There were no houses on the hill because it bordered a cemetery. The bus began to pick up speed and in order to keep up with it I hung onto a railing that covered the rear windows. As the bus went faster and faster I became very frightened and had no choice but to hang onto the railing. I hung on for dear life and thankfully made it to the bottom of the hill. The bus then slowly went a few more stops and my young friend, Dolores, disembarked. She was shocked to see me sitting there on my bike and admonished me for being so reckless. She did allow me to accompany her the rest of the way to her home. Ironically, it was closer to my home than to the White Castle. I could ride to her house on my bicycle from my house much more easily. I saw her more often after that and was then able to brag to my high school friends that I had a girlfriend. I met her mother one day when they came in together. I was allowed to visit her at home after that and we often spent the evenings playing records. That summer went by quickly and at the end of summer we both went back to school. I never saw her again, I assumed she was not interested in carrying on a relationship any more. I was unaware that she had met a marine and dropped out of school to get married. I was content to get on with my life. It had been a pleasant experience and I was feeling a bit cocky, having little trouble meeting other girls. I enjoyed those brief few months with Dolores. I had experienced my first close relationship with a girl and enjoyed it. We would never see each other again but forgetting her proved to be much more difficult than I thought at the time. Sixty-six years later I received a phone call asking if I was Gene Fagnano. When I replied yes, a female voice asked if I remembered Dolores from Ridgefield, NJ. I said I did. She said she was Dolores. She was calling from Florida and was wondering if I still lived in Fairview. I told her I was happily married, with two married children. She replied she was a widow also with two married children. We exchanged pleasantries for a few moments and I told her I was in good health but was scheduled for bypass surgery soon. She wished me well and apologized for the call and assured me she wouldn't bother me with any future calls. I thanked her and explained to my wife about the call. My surgery went well but the following year I lost my beloved wife. I then received another call from Dolores, she was just calling to see how I made out with my surgery. I said I was doing just fine but lost my wife. She was very touched by my loss and apologetic for bothering me. Her daughter took the phone and asked if it would be all right with me if her mom could keep in touch with me. I said if it helped her mother, now in her eighties, dealing with her life, I didn't mind. That resulted in weekly calls from Florida for a couple of years. Sadly she suffered a stroke and it became difficult to understand her. The last call I received was from her daughter with the news that she had passed away leaving me just another memory.

There were many other small incidents not worth mentioning during my time working at the Castle. Working there during my high school days became a real learning experience. I was able to take on a whole new identity. I no longer felt humble about my background and felt that I was part of a whole new environment. I developed many new friendships, both young and old. I no longer felt the inferiority complex I experienced as a younger teenager. Each one was a learning experience and I tried to benefit from them. As the war ended and my three brothers returned home, I had to fulfill my obligation to serve in the occupation forces.

And, I had just met the love of my life.

My first job, White Castle, North Bergen, 1943

The Post War Years

Suddenly, with the war ending, what had once been important events seemed like just fleeting moments. The family began emerging from their cocoons and like butterflies in the wind, they set out to explore a new world. Wedding bells began to ring and the Fagnano family grew with more celebrations.

First, my brother, Raymond, came home on leave and married his girlfriend, Margaret Shea. They moved in with her parents. As the war ended, my sister, Rita, married her boyfriend, Gene Campagna, who was the stepson of our old friend from Ohio, Tom Bruno. They went on to live with Gene's mother and stepfather in Brooklyn, New York. They soon moved back to New Jersey, lived in an apartment for a short while in Fairview, and then bought their home in the nearby town of Cliffside Park. My brother, Anthony, was discharged from the Navy, and married a neighborhood girl, Harriet Gratta, who was a friend of our sister, Rita. He decided to go to school under the G.I.Bill, became an auto mechanic, and went to work with our brother-in-law, Dan Verina. They moved in with her parents until they rented an apartment in Fairview on Park Avenue, next door to Adeline and Dan. A short time later they bought a home a few doors away. My brother, Albert and hiis wife had moved into an apartment in nearby Cliffside Park. All the weddings were happy occasions. The only one I missed was my brother Anthony's because I was away on basic training, beginning my tour of duty in the Army.

Meeting The Love Of My Life

Time has passed so quickly it's hard to remember the sequence of these events. But among all these memories is the one I will never forget, the day I met my future wife, Edna Koludrovich. She walked into the White Castle and straight into my heart. She was a fifteen year old high school student. I was then seventeen years old, a recent high school graduate waiting to enlist in the Army. I have since written in detail about our courtship in a book titled, "Prisoner Of Love." I will tell you now that the moment I first saw her I was smitten by her beauty. In story books, I have often seen eyes described as, "sparkling." Hers truly sparkled. After several bungling attempts to engage her in a conversation I was finally able to find out her name. I had never seen her before, she said she was from Hoboken, New

Jersey, and this was the first time she had ever been to this White Castle. It was the last two weeks of summer vacation and I thought I might never see this girl again. I begged for her address to no avail but she did say that she and her girlfriends might stop by one more time before school began again. All I could do was hope and pray I would get one more chance to see her. As she ran to the bus I took off my new graduation ring and pressed it into her hand. She had to catch the bus and had little time to protest my desperate gesture. Fortunately, she did come back the following week. But she returned my ring, explaining to me she was not allowed to date boys and it would be useless for me to try and see her again. She did give me her address but cautioned me about pursuing a relationship. Despite my frustrations and sense of hopelessness my romantic interest continued.

It would be months later, after a series of events, that I was able to see her again. While driving a taxi cab part-time, I picked up a fare to Hoboken. It was the first time I had ever visited Hoboken. When I realized I would be driving past her house I took advantage of the opportunity to drop a note into her mailbox asking her to please call me. I was running out of time before enlisting in the Army. After numerous phone calls, (Edna had no home phone, she would call from a pay phone) and much negotiating with her mother, she was given permission to see me just one time, in the afternoon while her father was at work. We were allowed to go see a movie at a theater just half a block from her house. As I tried to snuggle a little closer during the movie, my love cautioned me. I didn't realize that her mother was sitting behind us. From that day on there would be no separating us again. Although her mother told me I could not see her again we carried on by telephone for weeks. We began meeting each other secretly whenever possible. Time was running out, I had only a few months before leaving for the Army. We confessed to her mother that we were seeing each other and explained I would be leaving soon. Our courtship was fraught with complications. When I first told my mother about the beautiful girl I had just met, she didn't seem too concerned, until I mentioned the fact that I had given her my new graduation ring. That got her attention and she wanted to know more about the girl. We were devout Catholics and when I told Mama my new girlfriend was Lutheran, she just looked at me and frowned. When she asked what nationality Edna was, I knew I was in trouble.

I told Mama she was German and Yugoslav. As it was with many old time Italian families I knew my mother would have preferred I found a nice, Italian girl. There were plenty of Valsinnese girls available, and it would have made both my mother and my father very happy if I had found one I liked. I assured my mother she would like this girl once she met her. I invited my love and her mother to our home and it turned out to be a very pleasant meeting.

My mother was immediately impressed by both the beauty and personality of my new girlfriend. Her mother, who up till then still had serious reservations about allowing her daughter to date boys, agreed with my mother to allow us to date, with certain restrictions. We had only a few months to secure our relationship because of my commitment to serve in the Occupation Army, even though hostilities had ceased. We did not need months to get acquainted, it had been love at first sight and we made the most of it. She had to be home before nine o'clock at night, and we had to keep her father from finding out we were dating. Because I wasn't allowed to visit her home we spent most of our time at my home. She became part of our family and really enjoyed the company of all my brothers and sisters. She had only an older and younger sister, Gertrude and Irene, and one aunt and uncle nearby, Anna and Max. She was not used to all the activities around a large family but soon felt right at home with us. It was a whole new life for her and I could see she really wanted to be a part of it. She even became somewhat special to my father, he did have an eye for beauty. He loved all his daughters-in-law, but it was obvious she was his favorite.

Eugene & Edna

    I dreaded the thought of being separated for the year and a half of my enlistment, despite the assurances of my love that she would wait for me always. I thought of all the years my brothers had spent in the service during the war and felt guilty about complaining. I finally enlisted, hoping to get my service over with as soon as possible, and return to my one and only love. I was away for six weeks of basic training, and wrote a letter to my sweetheart every day. I received one from her every day. When my mother wrote to me, she often praised my girlfriend. Mama had become very fond of her and was teaching her to knit and cook Italian foods. My love visited her every Saturday and they would listen to the Saturday morning operas. Near the end of my basic training, in a foolish attempt to "play the martyr," I wrote my love a letter telling her she did not have to wait for me, and I would understand if she dated other boys. Of course, these were in no way my true feelings. I received two letters in a quick response. One was from my love, imploring me not to think that way and assuring me she would wait as long as it took to be together again. The other letter was from my mother, scolding me in no uncertain terms for upsetting my love. Edna had gone to my mother in tears and showed her my letter. Mama tried to convince her that I could not have meant what I wrote. There would be no more "playing games" with our love after that. I learned a lesson I never forgot and was quick to make amends. My mother attended my love's high school graduation ceremony and was quite impressed with all the awards she achieved and the scholarship she had been granted. She could not have been more proud had it been her own daughter. I felt sorry I could not be at the graduation, but was grateful my mother attended.

When my six-weeks training was up I came home on leave for one week, and it was love in full bloom. It felt like we had been separated for months. We spent every minute we could together and cemented what was already a lasting relationship. I went back to camp to await my reassignment, already thinking about my next furlough when I could see my love again. Happily, I did not have to wait too long. I had played trumpet in my high school band and a trumpet player was needed in the Army Band stationed an hour away from my home in Fort Hamilton, Brooklyn NY. I was transferred there and was able to come home several nights a week. My love and I resumed our courtship and patiently waited out the rest of my enlistment. My love turned down a scholarship she had received and instead went to work as a stenographer at a printing plant, Alco Gravure in Hoboken. With her exceptional skills she soon became secretary to the vice president, a position that would later afford me the opportunity to begin a career as a pressman with the New York Times.

The Crisis

The tranquility and optimism we had been enjoying up to this time was soon shattered in late July, 1947. I had just come home on a one day pass and stopped by my sister, Adeline's, house on the way home. I found her sitting at the kitchen table, crying. My brother-in-law, Dan, informed me that my father had just had a heart attack and was in the hospital. I ran home and found some of the family waiting to hear from the hospital, while others had already gone to the emergency room. In a little while we received a call from one of my sisters and were told that my father had survived the attack and was doing well. When I was able to visit him with my brothers, we found him in good spirits. His doctor assured us he would make a quick recovery. It was a shock to all of us, especially to our mother, she was visibly shaken. She had met many challenges before with courage and prayers, but this one would surely test her faith to the limit. As the crisis stage of this event eased, the reality of the situation became obvious. There was no way of telling how long it would take for my father to recuperate. He had three young daughters to support, still at home and in school, and I still had a month to go in my enlistment. The love of my life had been waiting for me to be discharged so we could become engaged and eventually married. There was no question now that top priority had to be given to the problems at home. My plans would have to be put on hold for a while.

My first task was to see if I could get an emergency discharge. I went through the proper channels to see if I could be discharged a month earlier than my enlistment. I obtained a letter from my father's doctor and another from the priest in our parish. I wrote a personal letter to my commanding officer asking for his assistance. My request was granted and a week later I was granted a dependency discharge. My next concern was to find a job as soon as possible. I would be the sole support for our family until my father fully recovered. Having no other experience other than my years working at the White Castle I had to entertain the thought of returning to work there. It was then that

I was given the opportunity of a lifetime that would change our lives forever. My love had become employed as a secretary for the vice-president of the Alco Gravure Printing Company in Hoboken, which was a satellite plant for the New York Times. As such, she became acquainted with various department heads. In the course of a conversation with the pressroom foreman, Joe Kilian, she mentioned that I was going to be discharged from the Army. He informed her that he was going to be hiring help soon and if I needed a job I should contact him. The job required joining the Newspaper Pressman's Union, and at that time it was a, "closed union," meaning you had to be related to someone in order to be accepted as a member. In a very kind gesture the foreman offered to sponsor me himself so I could be admitted to the union. The day after my discharge I reported for work at Alco Gravure, with no idea of what kind of work I would be doing. I knew it would be more of a career than I would have had at the White Castle. It was, in fact, the only job I would ever have. For forty-six years I worked my way from stacking newspapers to running a press. I eventually retired from the New York Times as a pressroom foreman.

My years as a pressman are another story, for now the dilemma my mother faced was all that concerned me. My father hired a barber to work at his shop while he was recovering, and I was making a fair salary at the time so we were meeting the challenge. Mama nursed and babied my father back to health and he was back to work sooner than we expected. My mother had climbed another mountain and remained steadfast in her faith. Unfortunately, because I was giving my mother most of my earnings, my thoughts of saving for an engagement ring and marriage were forgotten for the moment. My love kept on working and saving for both of us.

"Neither Rain, Nor Sleet"

I was becoming more frustrated in my desire to be with my love every day. On very rare occasions when we couldn't see each other I would become very anxious and despondent. It had reached a point where I was skipping meals and going without sleep to be with her every possible moment. While we were both working day shifts everything was fine. I was working the eight to four shift while she was working from nine to five. She would go home after work to change clothes, after which, we would usually meet at my house. Time always seemed to pass too quickly for me. Then we were forced to change our routine. I was transferred to the midnight shift and my hours were from twelve midnight until eight o'clock in the morning. When I finished my shift I was able to see her briefly before she left for work. I would then go home and sleep until Edna arrived at my house in the early evening. It became a problem when I did not get to bed on time but still wanted to be up when she arrived. I would often go without dinner so we could have time for a movie or other social activity. I began to lose weight and the lack of sleep made it difficult to get through a night's work. It was noticeable enough to cause my father concern. It was extremely rare for Papa to ever express an opinion on his childrens' personal lives. While watching television one evening he looked at me and asked what was troubling me. I was very surprised and assured him nothing was bothering me. He said I did not look well and was losing too much weight. He advised me to take better care of myself and stop being so obsessed with my love life. I was both embarrassed and shocked by his remarks.

Soon after, his words took on more meaning as a result of an unexpected snow storm. One morning, at the end of my night's work, I met my love as usual before she left for work, and said I would see her that evening. While I was sleeping it began to snow, and by the time I woke up, a foot of snow had already fallen. I wasted little time getting dressed, skipped breakfast and hurried to the bus stop. The snow was coming down steadily now and there was little traffic on the road. I waited quite some time for a bus and eventually decided to start walking toward the main bus stop about a mile away. Meanwhile, I had hoped a bus would come along, but not one did. When I reached the bus stop there were quite a few people waiting. Some had begun walking to the next bus stop and I joined them. Traffic had come to almost a standstill and people were walking down the middle of the street as the sidewalks had become impassable. As we trudged together, we began to talk and joke with one another. It soon became quite apparent that no buses would be coming our way. By this time I had walked a few miles and had to entertain the thought of turning around and going home. I kept on walking, calculating in my mind that I had probably walked almost halfway to Hoboken. The prospect of seeing my love that evening in spite of a snowstorm kept urging me on and I continued walking with renewed vigor. I had walked five-miles hikes in the Army and was beginning to feel the excitement about the challenge of walking all the way to Hoboken. Almost three hours later I arrived at my love's doorstep, having walked eight miles in over two feet of snow. She still had no telephone and had no expectations of seeing me that evening. The problem now was to let her know I was there. I was fearful her father might be home but took the risk anyway and rang the doorbell. When I was buzzed in I stepped onto the sidewalk instead of entering the building. After a few minutes, she looked out the window and saw me, came downstairs quickly, and after a very passionate greeting I explained the circumstances of my unexpected visit. We went across the street to our favorite luncheonette and I thawed out while we sipped hot chocolates. We sat a little longer than her nine o'clock curfew, and I decided to then go to work early so I could catch a few hours of sleep before my shift started at midnight. I still had to walk another half mile to the Alco Gravure plant since no buses were running. When I arrived at work my supervisor was standing by the time clock, patiently waiting for workers to arrive. He was both surprised and very happy to see me because half of the men had not shown up because of the weather. He was quite impressed with the fact that I reported to work, unaware of my ulterior motives. I did not get any sleep, but instead worked a ten-hour shift. I saw my girl the following morning before she left for work. The bus service had been restored and I then headed home for a much needed rest. I began to think about my father's warnings. The whole incident may have been foolish and irresponsible but at that time those few hours with my love were worth it. I was on the midnight shift for only a few more weeks and then returned to the day shift.

The front page of The Record,
Dec. 27, 1947
NorthJersey.com file photo

Although we had much more time to spend with each other now, we weren't completely comfortable with our situation. It was becoming very stressful hiding our relationship from my love's father. Her mother had accepted our relationship completely, and although we had her sympathy she was still reluctant to confront her husband. My love and I would continue dating secretly and she kept her pledge to be home by nine o'clock every night. I accepted and tolerated these conditions for about a year, then I finally convinced her and her mother it would be best if we resolved the matter once and for all. I asked for and received permission to meet her father and confess my relationship with his daughter. Meeting him face to face was more pleasant than I expected. Much to my surprise he was very understanding and after a man-to-man talk with him our problem was solved. Looking at me with a slight grin on his face, he said he'd known for quite some time what was going on. My future wife stood off in a corner of the room, visibly shaken, with tears in her eyes.

By now I had managed to save a little money, and with a small loan from my father after he returned to work, I was able to purchase my first used car. It was much easier now traveling back and forth to Hoboken to see my love and to go to work. It also gave us the opportunity to spend some time alone at last. We finally began to enjoy a normal courtship and I had a partner for life. We could now concentrate on our future plans. After two more years of working and saving we were finally married on September 10, 1950.

Edna's mother and father, Emma and Vladimir Koludrovich with Cindy

Our Wedding Day, September 10, 1950

Pictured with the wedding party are Edna's two sisters. Irene, seated, second from left, and Gertrude, standing.

My brother, Albert, and his wife had been living at home because apartments were scarce. They finally found an apartment nearby. My wife and I took advantage of the opportunity to move into my parents' house until we could also find an apartment. Edna enjoyed living with my mother and they bonded the mother-daughter relationship they had already possessed. I was able to help my father with the maintenance chores around the house. We finished the basement and built a little bar which received plenty of use later on with all the family gatherings.

Albert and Eugene at the bar we built

Dan Verina with Debbie

Papa dreamed of one day owning a small bar and grill. Mama would work the kitchen and Papa would work the grill with the help of his sons. He was serious enough about it to spend his day off searching in the newspapers for available locations. When he would find one that might be a possibility I would drive him there to look at it. We never found one he could afford but he kept looking and hoping. I must say I was looking forward to owning my own house someday, but I was really enjoying living at home with my parents and three younger sisters. It was a pleasure sitting and chatting with my father, and watching television together in the evenings. Television sets were not very reliable in those days so I was constantly adjusting the picture for him. Mama enjoyed sharing her skills at knitting and cooking with my wife who was even acquiring Italian mannerisms. My sister Dolores' boyfriend, Joseph Deery, came home from the Navy, and after a short courtship they were married and moved to his hometown in Pennsylvania. After we lived two years with my mother and father, an apartment became available in the same building where my brother, Albert, lived. My wife and I were elated and we quickly rented the rooms, leaving sisters Rosie and Frances the last two living at home. Meanwhile, we were also able to find an apartment nearby for my in-laws. So, for the most part, the Fagnano family was intact and for the next few years we all enjoyed living close together.

My first car - a 1937 Pontiac

The Tragedy

Suddenly, and without warning, the unimaginable occurred all too soon. At the age of fifty-nine, at three o'clock in the morning on July 30, 1953, my father suffered a fatal heart attack. He had been in good health and it was an unexpected shock to all of us. Within the hour everyone available had arrived at the house. My mother was inconsolable in her grief. For the first time in her life she had lost all faith. She had overcome challenge after challenge with her husband at her side. This time she was alone and helpless and unable to cope with the loss of her soulmate. It didn't seem fair, that after all they had been through together, it should end like this. It would be difficult for her to ever enjoy anything again without her lifetime partner. They had achieved all their goals but were denied the satisfaction of sharing them together. In her state of mind she was oblivious to what the future held for her. My father left no insurance policies and she would be living with two young daughters and no income in a house that was still mortgaged. My older brothers and sisters had to get together and decide what to do. None of us had any idea of what the barbershop was worth if we sold it. With the consent of my mother we decided to keep the shop and hire a barber to run it and share the profits with my mother. That only lasted a few months. The barber claimed that business had fallen off, and it wasn't worthwhile to keep it going. Reluctantly, we decided to sell it. That did little to solve the financial situation so we all agreed that each of us would chip in and give my mother a weekly allowance. This helped to sustain her for a while. Our youngest sister, Frances, married and moved into an apartment nearby. My sister, Rosie, became Mama's sole caregiver. Mama had lost complete interest in everything.

Life Without Papa

An event occurred which changed my life and also altered my mother's. She had been in deep mourning for over a year when my first daughter, Debra, was born on October 29, 1954. Mama already had ten grandchildren and with her depressed state of mind I didn't think one more would do anything to lift her spirits. Unfortunately, shortly after Debra was born, my wife suffered a case of postpartum depression. She was having a very difficult time nursing and caring for our baby. We had no choice but to seek help. I went to my mother and she suggested I bring my wife and baby to stay with her. I packed our necessary belongings and moved back home for several weeks. There was a remarkable change in my mother's demeanor. It had been a long time since she held and cared for a little baby. She had a renewed vigor and for the time being was her old self again. My sisters offered their help but my mother was in complete charge. It took a few weeks for Edna to recover from her ordeal. My mother was happy for my wife, but I think she was a little sad to see us return to our apartment. Seeing how much my mother enjoyed taking care of my wife and baby I tried to visit her as often as possible.

Our second daughter, Cindy, was born on November 13, 1957. We were still living in our apartment in Cliffside Park, with Albert, Margie, and their son, Mark, living in the apartment just below us. Raymond, his wife, Margaret, and their three children, Patty, Donna, and Raymond, lived around the corner. Eventually, Raymond bought a house further away in Rivervale. Dolores, Joe and their children, Jeanne, Karen, Gail, and Joseph, were still living in Levittown, Pennsylvania. Frances, Bill and their children, Theresa, Dawn, Renee, Billy, and John, were living about twenty minutes away in Rutherford, New Jersey. We all kept in touch with them regularly and they visited Fairview often.

There were many family gatherings…birthdays, First Communions, Confirmations, graduations, weddings, anniversaries, holidays. Actually, we didn't need special events to get together, it just became routine. It was during this era that the clock seemed to stop ticking and time stood still. The "rain" had ended and we were enjoying the inevitable rainbow. We enjoyed being close to each other, and still being close to our home on North 8th Street.

This is my painting of the view looking from Cindy's back door across my yard to Anthony's yard. Edna and Harriet are included in the picture.

Our house on Park Avenue

Life on Park Avenue

    In January, 1960, Albert bought a home on Park Avenue in Fairview, the same street where our sister, Adeline, and brother, Anthony, were living, and two blocks from Mama's house around the corner where we grew up. Then the house next door to Anthony and Harriet went up for sale. Edna and I bought it immediately and moved in on December 1, 1960. Mama now had three sons and a daughter close by, while our sister, Rose, her husband, Bert, and their son, Robert were living with her on North 8th Street. A few years later, Adeline and Dan's daughter, Daniella, bought a home with her husband, Joe, on our block. Their son, Michael, and his new bride, Lillian, moved into an apartment across the street. The years that followed are what made our family unique. While they were just fleeting moments in time, they created lasting memories.

Park Avenue sloped down, just past Albert's house, to North 8th Street. Mama had a daily routine of "walking up the hill" to visit her children and grandchildren. Our house was her last stop and she would enjoy staying a while to have a cup of tea and a little dessert with my wife, who always had a special place in her heart for my mother. Sometimes I would play Mama's favorite songs on my trumpet, often accompanied by Debbie on piano. She would pretend to keep time and occasionally would sing along. One day I began to play an old Italian song, "Mama," while she was talking to Edna. It is a beautiful song, but somewhat sad. She stopped talking, looked at me, and began to cry. After that, I played only tarantellas and popular songs. These were probably some of the happiest years of her life. Almost weekly, she would ask me to pick up a five pound bag of flour, a bag of potatoes, fresh spinach, and a gallon of oil. That meant everyone would soon be eating her delicious pizza and calzones. I was the delivery boy for whomever couldn't make it "down the house" and often brought some to the church rectory for the priests. Her talents in the kitchen led to her becoming a cook for the priests, a position she thoroughly enjoyed. Up until then my mother had always worn black clothing, which was customary among Italian widows. It was a pleasure seeing her wearing pretty, more modern clothing. Most surprisingly she had a new hairstyle replacing the bun she had worn since childhood. I often took her food shopping where she had the freedom to purchase all the ingredients she needed to cook her special meals. She was extremely proud when I was elected as councilman in town. The mayor and I had become very close personal friends and we often visited my mother's home. He would always greet her with a hug and a kiss. In between meals our priest, Father Florio, liked to stop and visit her which was always a pleasure for her. She was getting a lot of attention and she enjoyed every minute of it. Those five or six years helped her enjoy the life she always deserved. When it became apparent that the work was becoming difficult for her, Rose convinced her to retire and stay at home. She was finally content to sit back and enjoy the results of her faith and dreams. Eventually, the years of stress she had lived began to take their toll. Her health began to deteriorate and after a series of issues she was hospitalized. After several days, at the age of seventy six, she was gone. She was the glue that held the family together all these years. It was her courage and faith that was the guiding light that held our family together.

Bride, mother, and grandmother, she was truly a legend. If I was known as a "mama's boy" then I'm proud of it.

The Fagnano Boys and Their Antics

Growing up, Sundays were usually the most pleasant day of the week. It always began with reading the funnies in the newspaper after breakfast, a little music, and then later a pleasant meal. The afternoons were usually spent with visitors. One such morning began a little differently. Because there was always a scramble for the funnies, my brother Raymond and his friends decided to solve the problem their own way. The local Deli had a bundle of papers delivered every morning before they opened. One Sunday morning, Raymond and his friends stole the bundle. When we awoke, we found the papers all over the living room floor. They laughed and said, "Now everybody has the funnies!" When my father came downstairs to see what the commotion was about he was furious. He ordered me to gather up all the papers and bury them under the coal pile. Everyday after school I had to burn some until they were all gone.

Sometimes the antics were not quite so funny and were borderline illegal. One evening my brother Albert got a flat tire on his way home. Not having a spare tire he drove all the way home on the flat. By the time he got home he was riding on the rim of the wheel and it was flattened out completely. When Raymond and his friends became aware of the situation they went out to "find" another wheel. They returned a few hours later with a wheel and tire. Without Albert's consent or knowledge they found a car similar to Albert's and stole the wheel off the car. It soon became apparent that Raymond's friends were becoming a bad influence. They gradually cooled their relationship.

Of course, as time went on, the antics also continued. When Albert first moved into his home on Park Avenue, he became the recipient of one of our pranks. After he returned from the war, jobs were scarce so he decided to go to barber school and join our father at his barbershop. He worked at it only a few months and was not satisfied doing it for a living. He ended up accepting a chance to work for the A&P Company, where he remained until his retirement. However, he was the family barber up until his passing. He'd bring his tools to someone's house whenever needed and set up a one-night shop in the basement or garage, depending on the weather. My brother, Anthony, and I collaborated on welcoming Albert to Park Avenue by fashioning a barber pole from a long, cardboard tube. We painted it with red and white stripes, and Anthony found a light globe which he lit with a flashlight for the top. The night Albert and Margie moved into their house we put it on the front steps. We all celebrated their new home for a few hours until Albert went to the front door to let someone in. While we burst into laughter he just stood there, shaking his head. We thought he would be amused, but he wasn't. He was concerned about what the neighbors would think and it took some time to convince him they would appreciate the joke.

My brother, Anthony, loved hosting house parties. One time, a few weeks before Thanksgiving, he decided to have a gathering at his house. He often ended his festivities by raffling off a door prize, usually a bottle of cheer. Our sister, Rita's husband, Gene, made the mistake of commenting that in the past, he'd never won the prize. Anthony decided to rig this raffle so that he would win. Much to Gene's delight, he won, but the prize was not a bottle of cheer, it was a live turkey. Despite his protests, he had to take the turkey home with him. In the weeks that followed Gene and Rita kept the bird in their basement, at a loss for what to do with it. Unknown to them, Anthony had made arrangements with the poultry dealer to kill and dress the turkey for whoever won it. When it was finally revealed what the outcome would be I volunteered to bring Rita and the turkey to the market as planned. Their young son, Nicholas, had become attached to the turkey and Rita was not too happy about the whole event. I doubt they enjoyed their Thanksgiving dinner that year.

On one happy occasion, my brother Anthony, Daniella's husband Joe and I rushed Albert and his pregnant wife, Margie, to the hospital for the birth of their second child. While in the waiting room, Albert was admiring the paintings on the wall, Anthony and Joe were sipping coffee by the vending machine. I was pacing up and down because I had done the driving and was trying to calm down after having gotten there just in time. Soon the nurse, a nun, came in and looked around, then said to me, "You can come in now." I told her I wasn't the father and she asked who was. But before I could reply, our brother, Anthony, said, "We want to see who it looks like first." To make this story even more interesting, the baby, named Frank, actually resembled me more than he resembled Albert. The nun didn't seem amused while Albert sheepishly followed her out of the room.

Sometimes it wasn't a planned antic, but simply a big mishap. One afternoon my sister, Adeline, requested my presence at her house. Her husband, Dan, was home that day and decided to clean the house chimney. He devised what he thought would be the right implement to accomplish the chore. He stuffed a potato sack with old rags and tied it to a long rope. His intent was to drop it down the chimney and work it up and down. Adeline was concerned about him climbing on the roof and asked me to stop by and assist him. When I arrived, he was already on the roof and had begun the operation. I heard Adeline calling out to Dan in a panic from the basement, he evidently couldn't hear her. I called up to him and told him to hold on a minute as I ran to the basement. What I saw was a sight I will never forget. Adeline was standing next to the furnace, covered in soot. There was soot everywhere and it was slowly being drawn up the stairway through the upstairs rooms. I realized immediately that the attic fan was turned on and had been sucking the soot through the house and out the attic vents. My sister was in tears. When her husband came down from the roof and saw what had occurred he was devastated. It took many months and even some professional help to get the house back in order. But what had been a sad and unfortunate incident that day became the subject of many jokes during future gatherings at their home. Even Adeline found some humor in recalling the events of that day, and occasionally embellished the storyline somewhat.

No one was immune from the occasional practical joke. As noted before, Anthony was very skilled at making lawn ornaments. During the Christmas season he made four-foot wooden angel figures to adorn his front lawn. Our brother-in-law, Dan Verina, in a playful mood late one evening, painted mustaches on the angel faces. This was not discovered until the next day. Anthony took it all in stride and restored them. On another occasion, after remodeling his bathroom, Anthony put the sink out to the curb for disposal. It was a white porcelain sink shaped like a half-moon and I took a little creative license with it by placing it on end in his immaculate front yard. I had a small, decorative statue of Louis Armstrong, which I placed inside the bowl of the sink and adorned it with a few artificial flowers donated by my wife. I did not mean for this to be sacrilegious and I do not think it was taken that way. While some family members who were visiting that day sat out back on the patio, Anthony was inside his house gazing out the picture window, noticing how the people walking by would stop and point at his lawn, smiling. He remarked that he thought they were admiring his beautiful lawn and flowers. We all had to restrain ourselves from laughing and allowed it to go on for the better part of the afternoon. When a neighbor came from across the street with his camera, curiosity got the best of my brother and he stepped outside to talk with the neighbor. The neighbor said he just had to get a picture of that, and pointed to my creation. Anthony joined in on the laughter, probably planning something in retaliation.

The brothers - Eugene, Albert, Anthony, Raymond

Albert, Gene Campagna, Anthony, Bill Terrazzi, and Raymond

Togetherness was evident at all family gatherings. Whether it be sharing a happy occasion or dealing with a misfortune, the family stood united. Their fierce devotion to one another never wavered. All my brothers and sisters were individually talented, which made any get together a festive occasion. Anthony and Harriet were the hosts for many of these gatherings. In November, 1979, one of those misfortunes occurred during the night in my brother's backyard. His brand new car caught fire in the garage and both the car and garage were destroyed. Anthony possessed unusual skills at many different crafts….mechanical, electrical, carpentry, and enjoyed many hobbies. He made his own wine, and cultivated a beautiful vegetable garden every year. He always found time for his arts and crafts projects, such as building huge model airplanes and lawn ornaments. It was no surprise that he would rebuild the garage himself. It was amazing how he built it, and naturally, it became a family project, many of our relatives working together to complete the task. He designed the garage with a specific goal in mind. It was going to be the centerpiece of his backyard. He designed a two-car garage to replace the smaller one that had burned down. He built a ten-foot window on the patio side which opened up with an overhead electric door. On the inside he built a long wooden counter with four bar stools, and added a sink with hot and cold running water. Making the most of his skills and imagination he installed a gas restaurant-style grill. He covered the patio outside with a large, canvas awning. The whole project left nothing to be desired. During the summer months it became the central gathering place every Sunday. Pancakes, ham and eggs, hot dogs and drinks were served by our gracious hosts. Our brother, Raymond, would bring along a small electric keyboard, and our brother, Albert, and I would join in on sax and trumpet. Family members were often joined by friendly neighbors who would stop by. I lived next door and had a small swimming pool in the backyard, along with swings and playground equipment, all of which kept the children occupied while the grown-ups were entertained in Anthony's yard. These Sunday gatherings continued for many years. During the weekdays there were tea parties, sewing nights, and card playing at different homes where the women would gather and socialize. It was a lifestyle that had been instilled in all of us from our childhood. The tradition remained steadfast as our family grew and it was what made our family so special.

    Living so close to each other on Park Avenue, and so close to our family home a few blocks away on North 8th Street, we all became part of each other's daily lives. We not only shared the "special events" but also shared just everyday life. We lived like one big family all helping each other taking care of our homes and families, watching out for each other, making sure everyone had what they needed and sometimes just keeping each other company. This was important especially during the rough times. On three different occasions I had the unpleasant task of driving three of my nephews to their military recruiting centers. The first was my nephew, Joe Laino. He was recently married to Adeline's daughter, Daniella. I left her crying at home and he cried all the way to the Recruitment Center. Knowing how I felt when I had to leave my love I could sympathize with him. When I returned home after leaving him I was almost in tears myself. A short while later, Joe came bursting into my home. Laughing with joy he ran over and hugged me. I was speechless. He informed me that they had taken a second physical when they got to camp and he was rejected due to punctured eardrums. I watched as he ran down the block to his home, trying to imagine what his wife was going to feel when she saw him. Some years later, Adeline's son, Michael, was being sent to Vietnam. He did not want to go and on the way there he vowed he would find a way to come home. Thankfully, he returned home safely after his tour was over. The last to go was my nephew, Jimmie, Anthony's son. Unlike his cousins, Jimmie was anxious to go. He was always looking for excitement. He was in a very pleasant mood when I bid him farewell. After serving his time on the front lines in Vietnam, Jimmie signed on for another three years and was then stationed in Hawaii. He, too, finally returned home safely. The family had survived another few bumps along their paths to the rainbow.

When my daughter, Cindy, and her husband, Steve, moved in 1995 from Park Avenue with their five children we were sad to see them go. It was a difficult move for everyone involved but we all knew that they were moving to a place where their children would have excellent schools, and a big house in a safe, quiet neighborhood with a lot of property to spread out on. We were also happy that they would now be living less than five minutes away from my brother, Raymond, and his wife, Margie. My wife and I would take the drive up to their house on Sundays to visit and the jam sessions we always had on Park Avenue continued at Raymond's house. And now that I was retired, I would often bring my brother, Albert, for a drive up there during the week and he and Raymond and I would sit and play our music for a few hours. After a while, though, Albert's health declined and he couldn't make the trip. After dealing with surgery and hospitalization, my brother Albert passed away at the age of eighty-four.

Without my brother Albert playing his saxophone beside me I lost all interest in playing again. But when Raymond's wife told me how much he looked forward to my visits every Sunday and the little jam sessions we had, I felt obligated to keep playing with him. I made a practice of spending an hour or so each Sunday with him while visiting my grandchildren. Raymond's love of the piano helped him deal with our sorrow but at times it became difficult for me. My heart just wasn't into it. As time went on I noticed he was beginning to make mistakes while playing. I tried to relish anytime we had together fearing it might soon end. My fears were beginning to become a reality when he would tire in the middle of a session saying his hands hurt. I tried to cope with the thought that we were losing him by looking back at all the years we lived together. He enjoyed life, and even though he followed his own path he always remained close. He passed away at the age of eighty-eight after suffering a fatal stroke. The "Fagnano boys" were no longer the heart of the family.

After his passing, I put my trumpet back in its case vowing to never play again. But, later on, at my grandchildren's request, I began playing at their home during my Sunday visits. It brought back pleasant memories. When I could no longer play, I returned to my first hobby, painting, and began something new, writing.

Playing a band job - Eugene, Raymond, Albert

I will always take pride in being referred to as "one of the Fagnano boys".

Political Life

In December of 1960, when Edna and I moved with our two young children into our new house on Park Avenue in Fairview, I began my new job at the New York Times plant across the river in Times Square, New York City. The first six years were difficult, I was working the night shift. My wife had to adjust to my meal times and sleep times, while I had to adjust to a new job. After six years, I went over to the plant at Lincoln Center. In 1968, the company decided to open a plant in Carlstadt, New Jersey, a fifteen-minute drive from my house. Working the daytime shift afforded me more time for both family and friends. I was now able to attend Mass on Sundays and spend more time becoming involved in church activities. I became an usher and was appointed as a trustee of the church. I was able to meet many old friends from my school days. One friend, John Martino, had become a lawyer and judge. He came to visit me one day with news that he'd been approached to campaign for election as mayor of Fairview. He asked if I would be his running mate. I was completely surprised, I had never been interested in politics. He explained that he wanted to run with someone who was new but who was also well known in town. I talked it over with my wife, who left it up to me to decide. My ego got the better of me and I agreed to join him. We were elected that year and I was elected to three more terms after that. John was a lawyer and a former judge and, like me, he had no experience in politics. Neither of us was interested in pursuing a career in politics. Most of the older politicians had businesses in town and were able to profit by their position in politics. My main goal was to deliver the services that taxpayers deserved. With the mayor's approval I started by rebuilding the children's playground with new equipment. I appointed a recreation committee to advise me of any further improvements we could make. The mayor then appointed me chairman to the Department of Public Works where I was able to make some real improvements. I began by purchasing equipment the department never had. I bought a leaf collector, a salt spreader and a new dump truck. The town was responsible for clearing all public sidewalks of snow. They used to send two men to shovel the snow by hand. I bought a large snow plow just for that purpose much to their delight. Sadly one day, both suddenly and unexpectedly, the mayor died from complicated issues. It was a complete shock to everyone. I was devastated, having lost my sidekick and friend, and dreaded the thought of finishing my term without him. While he was mayor, we had appointed Mike Rossi, a young man who had grown up in our neighborhood, as borough attorney. He accepted the offer to run for mayor if I would run for re-election with him. Very reluctantly I agreed and we were elected by a landslide. As our new mayor, Mike was extremely competent and brought many goals of his own with him. I continued to strive to improve our town and the services it provided to the residents. Once again with the mayor's approval, I bought a brand new garbage truck and after years of hiring outside trash collectors we now had our own trash removal service which really saved the town a lot of money. At the time, our council chambers had been located in an old converted bank. The mayor gave me permission to install offices which brought our town up to date with the surrounding towns. One of the services in town was transporting people to the hospital when needed. The ambulance was always driven by a police officer. I assisted in establishing a volunteer ambulance corps and bought a new ambulance. I had the much coveted role as police commissioner and my responsibilities with that took priority. We did not have a Housing Authority so I convinced the mayor we should join the Bergen County Housing Authority. We did and a few years later I was honored to be appointed as a commissioner to the Authority. I enjoyed the role of providing housing and assistance to hundreds of senior citizens. When the mayor was appointed a county judge I finished my term on the council and left politics but continued with my service with the housing authority. I served on the board for twenty years, the last ten as chairman. Years later a friend of mine asked me to enter politics once more and run with his young son hoping my popularity would help his son get elected. I agreed to just one more time. We were elected but by that time the opposing party had taken over the government in Fairview. Although, I got along very well with the new mayor even though we were from opposing parties. I finished my three year term and retired from politics for good.

My father taught me at a very early age that your name meant everything in life. He cautioned me to never do anything to dishonor it. On any occasion when I had to introduce myself, I was always proud to say, "I'm a Fagnano". To me it was like a "Badge of Honor".

Seated: (left) Mike Rossi, mayor-elect and (right), Mayor John Martino
Standing: (left) Al Festini and (right) Eugene Fagnano, councilmen elect

Adeline Verina, chairwoman of the Heart Fund, with Eugene Fagnano, co-chairman, and Mayor John Martino

Photo shows first Senior Citizen making rent payment to Councilman Eugene Fagnano, chairman of the Senior Citizens Rent Subsidy, executive committee.

My Years as a Pressman

Alco Gravure

The years I worked at Alco Gravure in Hoboken were so unique they seem unbelievable. I spent a good part of my life there preparing for the future. I started working there when I was nineteen years old, and I left at the age of thirty-four. My first few years involved mostly keeping the floors clean and later on catching newspapers off a conveyor belt and stacking them. It was a tedious task and not what I expected I would be doing. I was then given the opportunity to operate a lathe machine. It was one of the most sought-after jobs I held. For the next ten years I had plenty of free time and spent much of it watching and learning. Long before I received my Pressman's Card I knew my job well.

I became good friends with Oliver Bass, a boy who worked as the clerk in the pressroom office. He was a very good ball player and we decided to organize a softball team. We found enough interested boys in the various departments to form a pretty good team. We played ball against some of the other industrial teams after hours. We practiced every day on our lunch hour and pretty soon we were a formidable team. With Ollie as our captain we won several first place trophies. The office supervisors were very proud of our achievements and built a special case for the trophies in the main office.

Our softball team at Alco. My friend Ollie Bass is fourth from the right, peering over from the back

We were one of the few teams without uniforms, so one day I asked the boss if the company would allow us to put a couple of vending machines in the breakroom. We would use the profits to buy team uniforms. We received permission for a candy and cigarette machine, and soon had enough money for uniforms and jackets. We were still making money with the machines so we bought a lot of equipment - balls, bats, gloves and catcher's equipment. For the pressmen we bought a dartboard, checkers and chess games for the smoke room. Outside the side door of the pressroom there was an empty field of weeds. There was a track for the freight trains running through there and along the outskirts of Hoboken. On Saturdays the presses weren't running and it was "clean up" day for the boys. We cleared out a space on the field and put up a volleyball net and a pit for horseshoes. During the summer we all had our lunch outside. Taking advantage of the cooperation we received from our foreman we decided to build a barbecue. The maintenance man supplied the bricks and cement and the machinist made the grills. We began taking our cars back there and one of the boys kept his trunk open and had beer and soda in there. We got to know the engineer of the train as he passed by everyday. He had to go very slowly through the town and he would blow his whistle and wave and we would wave back. One Saturday, while we were enjoying a barbecue, he stopped the train and laughingly shouted down to us asking "Do you guys really get paid for that?" We shouted back, "Yeah, would you like a hot dog?" He said sure, and one of the boys climbed up the side of the engine and handed him a beer and a hot dog. He said thank you, then blew his whistle and went on his way.

At one time, I decided to try out some of the Fagnano humor on my coworkers, but ended up paying an unexpected price. While I was keeping company with my future wife, I confiscated a bottle of perfume she had discarded and brought it to work with me. During the day, as I came in contact with several of my fellow workers I managed to sprinkle them with a few drops of the perfume as they walked by. After a few hours, the pressroom began to smell like a flower shop. Then I got a little too careless and one of the men caught me. We all laughed it off and I thought I had gotten away with something, until the next day on my lunch break. I was driving Edna and two of her friends to lunch, as I often did. I had driven only a few blocks when suddenly my car filled with an odor beyond description. The girls quickly rolled down all the windows but no one said anything. I dropped them off at their destination and noticed a slight wisp of smoke coming from the engine. I opened the hood of my car and found the source of the odor. My coworkers had rubbed Limburger cheese on the exhaust pipe. As soon as the engine heated up the odor was unbearable. I tried every cleaning solution I could think of but it took a long time before the odor was completely eliminated. I had a talent for drawing caricatures and I used it for years to come as a form of retribution by drawing many of them in cartoons. These would be hung on the printing presses where they worked, much to the delight of the men I spared.

Restroom humor was very common in the pressroom. One day one of the boys brought in a clothes mannequin. We dressed it in work clothes while trying to decide what to do with it. The first time we used it was one morning right after coffee break, when the restroom was usually busiest. Our men's room had only two toilets. One of the boys sat the mannequin on a toilet and crawled out from under the door. The pants and shoes were clearly visible from under the swinging door. Ollie and I watched as the men patiently waited for the one booth to become available. As the line became longer, the men began to grumble until finally one of them went into the other booth, stood on the toilet and looked over to see if the person was all right. There was a little light-hearted laughing and the boys retreated. The mannequin next came out when one of the boys decided to go home for lunch one day. We knew he kept some beer in the trunk of his car which wasn't locked. We stuck the mannequin in the trunk with the legs hanging out. We all waited for him to come back from lunch to see what he had to say about the joke. Surprisingly, he said nothing. He had driven home and back and never knew it was there. He said he wondered why when a school crossing guard who stopped him to let the children cross the street gave him a strange look as he pulled away. The next time the mannequin surfaced it almost got us in trouble with our boss. One of the supervisors used to come down to the pressroom every morning to check in with our boss. The boys laid the mannequin on a platform near the bosses office and covered him with paper. It looked like somebody sleeping on the job. When our boss uncovered the mannequin the supervisor did not appreciate the joke. Pretending to be angry, my boss ordered the boys to get rid of the mannequin and told the supervisor he would take care of the matter. The mannequin was finally put to rest.

As time went on, one by one the boys left the Alco. Little by little the festivities ended with the arrival of new employees. But Ollie and I managed to work together until our retirement forty-four years later.

After fourteen years I finished my apprenticeship working at Alco and was promoted to Pressman. At the time there were no openings for pressmen at Alco. I was given the opportunity to choose any newspaper in our union in need of a pressman. There were five major newspapers in New York at the time. My boss assured me as soon as there was an opening he would welcome me back to Alco. He suggested I go to the New York Times where they always had openings. I took his advice and went to the Times. I joined my friend Ollie who had already gone there and soon learned there was a big difference between newspaper printing and the color presses I had trained on. I had to learn all over again.

The New York Times

It was 1960 when I went to work for the New York Times in New York City. I worked for six years in Times Square and then another two years in Lincoln Center. Working at the Times was a far cry from working at the ALCO. The pressroom was two stories underground and stepping off the elevator felt like entering a coal mine. The ceilings were very low, the noise was deafening and there was ink mist spread all over. Because it was night work most of the men spent a lot of their time smoking and drinking. They played card games all night in the locker room. We were assigned to work with different crews every night. It was difficult to have one steady partner to work with. Newspaper presses were much different than the color presses I trained on at Alco and it took a while to learn their operation. Ollie worked at the opposite side of the pressroom and we didn't get to see each other very often. The fun and games I had enjoyed for so many years were over. I began to doubt if I wanted to do this the rest of my life. I tolerated it for the next six years, praying for a chance to return to Alco. My luck changed when the Times decided to open a new pressroom in Lincoln Center, away from Times Square. They asked for volunteers to transfer there and I immediately gave my name. Many of the men chose to stay where they were because they had become used to their job. The new place was beautiful. It was a pleasure going to work everyday. I worked with the same crew every day and made many new friends. After two years I received a phone call at home from my old boss at Alco. He told me he had an opening for a pressman and asked me if I would come back. He said he would make me a foreman within six months. With so many men ahead of me at the Times I doubted that I would ever be a foreman there. Just the thought of returning to my old job really excited me. I told him I definitely would enjoy working there again, but I wanted to talk to my wife first. When word spread around that I might be leaving the Times I received all kinds of advice. Most of the men thought I would be foolish to leave. Many of my friends tried to discourage me, especially my friend, Ollie. I was surprised when one of the foremen came to me and said he heard I was leaving. He was one of the old timers and I had never gotten to know him very well. I was surprised he took an interest in me. He said, "I've been watching you, you're a good pressman and I hate to see you leave." He said, "You have a good future here, and Alco might not always be there. After work I went to look over the situation at Alco. It was a little disheartening. I had been gone eight years and many of the men had aged. I received a warm greeting as I walked among them until I went to see my old friend in the machine shop. He said "Gene, I hear you're thinking of coming back." I said "Yes, I am." He said, "I would be happy to see you again, but don't do it." A little confused, I asked why he said that and he warned me that Alco was going to close shop soon. They weren't even making repairs or ordering new parts anymore. I was shocked to hear that because I always thought Hoboken was their flagship plant. It concerned me enough to think twice about taking the job and I ultimately decided not to. Six months later the Alco Gravure closed its doors.

During the first few years working for the Times I wasn't familiar with the parking regulations in NY so I commuted by bus. At the time I was still working the night shift. One evening while standing at the bus stop with several other people waiting for the New York bus to arrive, a funeral hearse stopped for the red light. The weather was a little misty so it was difficult to see the driver. Suddenly we could make out a hand motioning from the window for someone to approach the car. Everyone looked at one another waiting to see who would move. Finally the window rolled down and a voice called out, "Gene". I approached the vehicle and recognized the driver. He offered me a lift, but I replied, "No, thanks, I'm going to New York". He said he was too, so I got in, much to the relief of the other people standing on the corner. He told me he was on his way to their other establishment in lower New York. I said he could drop me off outside the tunnel, since it was only a block or two from there to the Times, but he said he would bring me right to the door. When we pulled up in front of the Times building there were a few dozen men outside waiting to start the next shift in a few minutes. Suddenly, they all seemed to stop talking, staring at the hearse thinking it was there to pick up somebody. Some men even took their hats off. When I stepped out of the vehicle, there was a little bit of giggling and then laughter as the men recognized me. It was the topic of conversation for a long time afterwards.

As time went on I settled down to learning my trade and raising my family. Every now and then I would get a twinge of mischief thinking of the "old days" with Ollie. Occasionally, it got the best of me. There was an agreement with the Times saying that because of safety regulations, they would provide all the pressmen with two pairs of steel-toed shoes every year. One day, I watched as one of my co-workers who got dressed in the same aisle as me unwrapped a new pair of shoes. He put them on and threw his old shoes in the garbage. When I was leaving work that afternoon I took his old shoes from the garbage and put them on the bench by his locker. The following morning I watched when he came to his locker to get dressed. He stared at the shoes for a few seconds, then shook his head and again threw them in the garbage. This time he covered them up with old newspapers. At the end of the day I repeated what I had done the day before, and placed the shoes on his bench again. I made sure to be there a little early so I wouldn't miss when he came in. When he saw the shoes he looked around for a few minutes, brought them to the garbage can and threw them in again. I was satisfied that the joke had gone far enough. While we worked together that day he never mentioned the incident. The next morning, when I reported for work, I found my locker covered with black ink. We smiled at one another and returned to work as usual. No words necessary.

Our office boy became the recipient of some of our old "Alco humor". Whenever we had the opportunity, either my friend Ollie or I would rub a little black ink on the earpiece of the office telephone. We would then return to our presses and find an excuse to call the office. Unaware of our mischief, the clerk would answer the phone. It usually took a while before he became aware of what we had done. The first few times he took it all in good stride, and when it became annoying, we devised a new prank to play.

At that time, radios had tubes. When the radio was turned on it could sometimes take almost a minute before the sound could be heard. The clerk had a small radio in the office that they used for weather reports. Anytime I had reason to be in the office, on my way out I would turn the radio on to top volume and then quickly exit. I would be outside the door in time to watch the clerk leap out of his chair when the radio would come on full blast.

Traditionally, all the men in the pressroom wore paper hats that we made to protect our hair from the ink. One of my partners used to enjoy slapping me on the head and crushing my hat as he walked by. After tolerating his actions for quite some time I decided to put an end to it. I inserted a thumb tack on the inside of my hat then anxiously waited for the next time he "playfully" slapped me on the head. The next day I watched with anticipation as he approached me, unaware of the surprise I had waiting for him. As expected, he smiled and then slapped my head. He accepted the brief pain he endured and that was the last of the incidents involving my hat.

I received a real blessing when the Times decided to open another plant in Carlstadt, NJ, just fifteen minutes from my home. By then I had enough priority to work the day shift. There was nothing more I could ever wish for. The new pressroom was a modern and beautiful plant. I was enjoying my job at the new plant, close to home, and was happy to finally not have to travel into the city anymore. I learned my job very well and took great pleasure in passing on my knowledge to the younger workers. My deeds did not go unnoticed. My boss called me into his office one day and offered me a foreman's position. It meant a big raise in salary but it also meant working nights again. I was anxious to tell my darling about the offer. She was very emphatic about me refusing the job. She did not want to go through what she did when I worked the night shift before. She was very happy with the way things were and she begged me not to do anything to change it. My boss was a little disappointed but I told him I would keep on helping him any way I could.

A year later I had occasion to solve a little problem we were having in the pressroom. In gratitude the company told me to take my wife out to dinner at their expense. It also prompted my boss once more to ask if I would accept the foreman's position. This time my wife became a little upset, thinking I was going to accept the offer. The thought of sitting in an office instead of a pressroom was beginning to appeal to me. It meant no more noisy presses, no physical work, and wearing clean clothes. However, it still required working on a different shift. I had only a few more years until retirement. I had no problem with satisfying my wife's wishes. The offers finally came to an end the following year. I was summoned to the office, where there were several executives sitting there with my boss. He informed me that they were planning on building a new plant in Edison, New Jersey, about forty minutes from my home. I was offered the foreman's position once again, and was asked if I would accept it. I would be in charge of the installation of the new presses and it would be on the day shift. This was a really big challenge and I was anxious to take it on. This time my wife said it was up to me. I agreed to accept the position with the understanding that as soon as the last press was up and running I could retire. I began training men on the installation of the new presses. It took two years to complete the task. A celebration was held which was a very rewarding and proud moment for me and was attended by many dignitaries. After the ceremony for the start-up of the last new press I emptied my locker and retired with forty-six years of memories.

As foreman, I was in charge of the installation of six of these printing presses for the New York Times plant in Edison. Completion took two years - a task I promised to complete before retiring.

Me with my first crew of trainees and my pressroom supervisor, Frank Chimento, at the Edison plant

Me with my crew on the day of my retirement from the New York Times in Edison

Our Children

Debra Louise
October 29,1954

A new life began when our first daughter, Debra Louise, was born after thirty-six hours of labor, while I was pacing the floor. During the first few weeks with a new baby my wife suffered postpartum depression, so we stayed with my mother, who welcomed us eagerly. After we brought her home, I tried to be helpful to my love, but spent every minute I could with Debbie. She quickly became "Daddy's Little Girl." As she got older, I would often take her to Mama's house where she could play in the yard and visit the neighbors. She had a little pedal go-kart to ride up and down the driveway, and a tricycle. I built a child-sized picnic bench with an attached sandbox. The neighbors' children would often come over to play with her. Doting on Debbie soon became a problem. When I would come home from work she wanted my undivided attention. If I had to leave the apartment, she would cry until I returned. On one occasion, I foolishly came home for lunch. Debbie cried hysterically when it was time for me to leave. Any attempts to calm her down failed. I had no choice but to bring her back to work with me, not knowing how I was going to handle the situation when I got there. I could not keep her in the pressroom with me. Fearing the worst from my boss when I explained what was happening, he smiled and said, "Don't worry, we can take care of this." I had two hours left until quitting time and was deeply concerned as to how this was going to turn out.

My boss invited Debbie into his office and seated her at his desk. He gave her a notepad and crayon and told her to draw pictures. As different workers came in and out of the office they became amused at the sight of this little girl sitting at the boss's desk. Soon they were bringing her candy bars from the vending machine and some even gave her money. The nurse brought Debbie to her office for a while, too. Thankfully, time went by quickly and we returned home, much to the relief of my darling wife, with many stories to tell. A similar situation arose one night as I was leaving to bowl in a shop tournament. Once again, Debbie came with me, sat at the table and pretended to keep score, much to the amusement of my fellow bowlers.

As an infant and toddler, I brought Debbie with me to choir rehearsals at Our Lady of Grace Church in Fairview, until I began working the night shift and could no longer sing in the choir. Everyone would fuss over her, she was even allowed to sit beside the organist on the organ bench. This was to become a major influence in her life later on. At an early age Debbie showed signs of musical talent, sitting at the piano and playing little melodies that I taught her. At the age of seven she began formal piano lessons, which she continued into her studies at Jersey City State College. Since my church did not have a school, Debbie attended the grammar school a few blocks away at St. John the Baptist Church in Fairview. It was there that she joined the children's choir at the age of ten, and a few years later the organist, Barbara Mehr, took Debbie under her wing and opened the door to a lifetime career in liturgical music, as an organist, choir director and director of music. Her piano lessons led her to the entertainment industry, where she became a professional pianist in New Jersey. She also taught music in the Catholic Schools system until moving away. In 1980, after visiting New Orleans a few times, she met and married Jim Black, Jr., the bass player with trumpeter Al Hirt's jazz band. They then decided to move back to Jim's native Houston, Texas. Their son, Eugene, was born in 1981. Debbie continued with her church music and became a founding member of the Piano Entertainers Guild. In 1988, Jim was invited to rejoin Al Hirt's band, so they moved back to New Orleans. Debbie continued her church music, taught piano lessons privately, and performed at different venues in metro New Orleans. And then, in need of a piano player, Mr. Hirt hired Debbie for the position. I had the extreme pleasure of seeing her perform several times during her tours with the band. On one occasion, in Atlantic City, I had the opportunity to stand backstage while she played her featured solo. She received a standing ovation and Mr. Hirt said to me, "She can really play that thing." Jim and Debbie performed in New Orleans and traveled with the band for several years. Then Jim left the band to play with another group. After a friendly separation and divorce, Jim eventually went back to Houston, where he passed away in 2017.

An exciting and unusual position Debbie has held since 1989 is being the official calliope player on the Steamboat NATCHEZ, one of the major tourist attractions in New Orleans. Nicknamed "Ms.Calliope," she performs several fifteen minute concerts a day, sending up puffs of steam with each very loud note, welcoming passengers aboard. Debbie has also had appearances in TV shows, commercials, videos and documentaries about the steamboat and life in New Orleans. Since 2001, she has been the organist and Director Of Music Ministry at Our Lady Of Perpetual Help Church in Belle Chasse, LA. After many years, Debbie still loves what she is doing and has given me much to be proud of. She set a course early in life and has followed through with faith and determination.

Debbie has also inherited her mother's love for cooking, baking, sewing and crocheting. She learned to thread a needle before she started school and even knew what to do with a pair of knitting needles. She loved to spend time with her mother in the kitchen, and now enjoys hosting dinner parties for friends at her home. In recent years she has finally fulfilled her desire to travel, having made several solo journeys to Italy. It was an overwhelming experience for her to find the house in the medieval village, Valsinni, where Papa was born, and the current owner has made her home available to Debbie when she visits. The people of Valsinni have continued to welcome her with many, "baci e abbracci," kisses and hugs.

Having two professional musicians for parents, my grandson, Eugene, "Gene," Black, became a very talented musician. He began Suzuki violin lessons at the age of two, and continued until moving to New Orleans. There, he began private piano lessons. In high school, he became a drummer, and then picked up his father's upright bass and mastered the instrument. He performed with his father, Jim, in the jazz band on board the Riverboat CREOLE QUEEN, until the 2005 hurricane. He is currently a professional bassist and drummer in New Orleans, and teaches at the New Orleans Jazz And Heritage Foundation's School of Music.

Debbie playing the calliope on the Natchez

Eugene

Cindy Louise
November 13, 1957

    Cindy was born three years after our daughter, Debbie. Three years later we bought our home on Park Avenue and soon after I became a pressman at the New York Times. It meant a substantial increase in my salary but it required me to work nights for the next six years. Working nights, I could not spend the time with Cindy as I did with our first child, Debbie. Cindy quickly got used to spending time with other family members. She would go into anyone's arms and it was not unusual for someone to come and ask if they could take her for a walk in her carriage, often Uncle Dan or Grandpa. Because of the circumstances at the time, Debbie had become "daddy's little girl". Now, Cindy, as the baby of the family, had become "everyone's" little girl. While growing up, the two sisters became very attached to each other. Cindy loved all things in nature and has always had a special fondness for animals, especially rabbits. Like Debbie,

Cindy was an excellent student and enjoyed many talents. She had a gifted voice and learned to play the piano. But Cindy was never one to display her talents. Rather than follow in her sister Debbie's footsteps she was content to pursue her own dreams. She attended St. Joseph's High School in West New York and it was there that she met her first and only boyfriend, Steve Petrocelli, a boy from the town next to ours, Cliffside Park. Steve also was part of a large family of nine siblings. He was a good student, an athlete and a hard worker. They spent most of their time together, and by the time they graduated high school it was obvious that they were committed to staying together. I was very pleased with the choice Cindy had made. I had reservations about them marrying too soon, so when Steve respectfully asked me if they could become engaged, I gave him my permission with the understanding they would complete their college education. Cindy was a pleasure to counsel, always willing to accept the standards I had set for raising a family. She graduated from college with honors and immediately began teaching in Our Lady of Grace School in Fairview. They were married that same year in November, 1979, and rented an apartment across the street from the school. I was relieved she would still be nearby. Steve began working for a builder in North Jersey and soon after that began his own business in contracting and construction. He has earned an excellent reputation for both his craftsmanship and business management.

One day my next door neighbor visited me. He informed me he was thinking of selling his home. Knowing I might be in the market for a house he gave me first choice. At first I was excited about the thought of having my daughter living right next door to me but I realized the price he was asking is very high. Unable to get the price he was asking for, he decided to rent the home. After several tenants he realized the home was becoming an expense. Desperate to sell he came back with a very low offer. We quickly accepted it and Cindy and Steve bought the house. I have to pause here because there are no words to describe the next fifteen years. I now had my brother living on one side of my home and my daughter living on the other. Cindy fulfilled her dreams of having a large family and over the next seven years she and Steve welcomed the births of five children, three girls, Emma, Sara, and Amelia and two boys, Sam and Luke. Without a doubt, these were the happiest days of my life. It was inevitable Cindy and Steve would need a larger home to accommodate five children. I dreaded the thought of them moving and prayed that they would find a home nearby. All five of their children were now in school so a good school system was a high priority. They chose a town about a half hour away that had one of the highest school ratings in the state. It was a bit of an affluent town but they managed to find a home which was reasonably priced, a large home with a spacious rear yard. Steve used his skills and built a large addition to the home. Although my darling and I missed them very much, we enjoyed our weekly visits and were happy to see them in such a beautiful home. And, as it happened, they were now living just five minutes away from my brother, Raymond, and his wife, Margie, so we enjoyed seeing more of them also. As their children grew, Cindy became active in the church and school. She spent a number of years teaching religious education and also served as the director for the women's retreats. As they entered high school she became very involved with the music department, volunteering many hours as a staff assistant and as a committee member of the Music Parents Association. She volunteered as a chaperone for music festivals for many years, traveling the east coast with groups of hundreds of students. She also became a member of the production staff for the Musical Theater Department, working with faculty and students to design and create set dressings and stage properties for their elaborate productions - a position she enjoyed for twenty years. At the same time, Cindy became employed in the library of their local school system where she is still working. Steve still maintains his own construction business, though he is presently nearing retirement.

With five married children and ten grandchildren their home has become a gathering place reminiscent of my early years. All their children live nearby, and, having completed higher education they are all enjoying successful careers. Emma teaches art in her public school district and she and her husband, Chris Harvey, own and operate a well-established art studio in Bergen County. They have three sons, Vincent, and twins William and Anthony. Sara and her husband, Chad Armstrong, are both professional opera singers and have performed all around the United States and in Europe, most recently with the Metropolitan Opera in New York City. They also teach vocal music privately from a studio in their home. They have two children, Iris and Theodore. Amelia taught High School Mathematics and then advanced her education further and became the District Supervisor of

Mathematics in a nearby district. Her husband, Thomas Bowers, is a Physical Therapist. They have three children - Eleanora, Rosalie, and Thomas. Sam completed degrees in robotics and engineering and is currently a Software Engineer. His wife, Bridget (Baudinet), is an English and French language teacher. They have a daughter, Adeline, and are anxiously awaiting the arrival of their second child. Luke and his wife, Sarah (Stein), are both Architects and own and operate their own architecture practice in Brooklyn, NY. He is also currently teaching Architecture at New Jersey Institute of Technology. They have a daughter, Mila. They all have begun to carry on our traditions with growing families of their own.

Up until recently I had been living alone in my home since the loss of my darling wife. Cindy would come weekly to shop for groceries, clean the house, do laundry and take care of my needs. And, with all the help I received from my niece, Daniella, and her husband, Joseph Laino, I had been able to get by. They would check in on me every day to see if I needed anything. Daniella would cook meals for me and each evening Joe would walk up the street to deliver it to me with a smile. Their kindness was overwhelming and it was always comforting to know that they were close by. We will be forever grateful to them. Two years ago after I was hospitalized for pneumonia, my daughter Cindy suggested I stay with her while recovering. After a short while it became obvious that I would not be able to manage living on my own any longer, so we agreed that I should stay with them permanently. She and Steve have done much to make my stay with them pleasant and comfortable, rearranging their home to accommodate me and all my needs. Living with their family has given me the desire to welcome each new day as a gift. I am surrounded by my grandchildren and great-grandchildren. Cindy and Steve have made me feel I am no burden. As an elderly person with elderly needs I have been the recipient of the same love, affection and care all their little children enjoy. Having Cindy as a caretaker has given me the opportunity to write this book. I wish there was a Cindy in everyone's family.

After losing the love of my life, my wife Edna, I wrote a book titled "Prisoner Of Love" named after a popular song at the time of our courtship. It became our personal love song. Over the years the song has been mostly forgotten but it has always been a memory for me. An incident that Cindy and I shared somewhat recently leads me to believe I am not the only one who recognizes the role she has played in my well-being. A few years ago during a visit to the cemetery I watched as Cindy cleaned and decorated my wife's plaque. She will often use her phone to play music when visiting her mother and this time, since we were together, she played our song, "Prisoner Of Love". I listened to it with mixed feelings. When she was finished we returned to her car and headed home. The radio was playing some soft music. Suddenly, Cindy looked at me and gasped "Dad!", as she turned up the volume. The radio was playing the song "Prisoner Of Love." We were both struck speechless. I hadn't heard that song played on the radio for many years. We drove the rest of the way home in silence.

Coincidence? Omen? Message? Who knows. Food for thought.

Sara, Luke, Amelia, Sam, & Emma

From Left: Chris, Emma, Chad, Sara, Steve, Cindy, Tom, Amelia, Luke, Sarah, Bridget, Sam

And the family continues to grow……

From left: Eleanora, Mila, Anthony, Rosalie, Theodore, Adeline, William, Vincent, Thomas, & Iris

Watching Looney Toons with Pop-Pop on a Sunday Afternoon

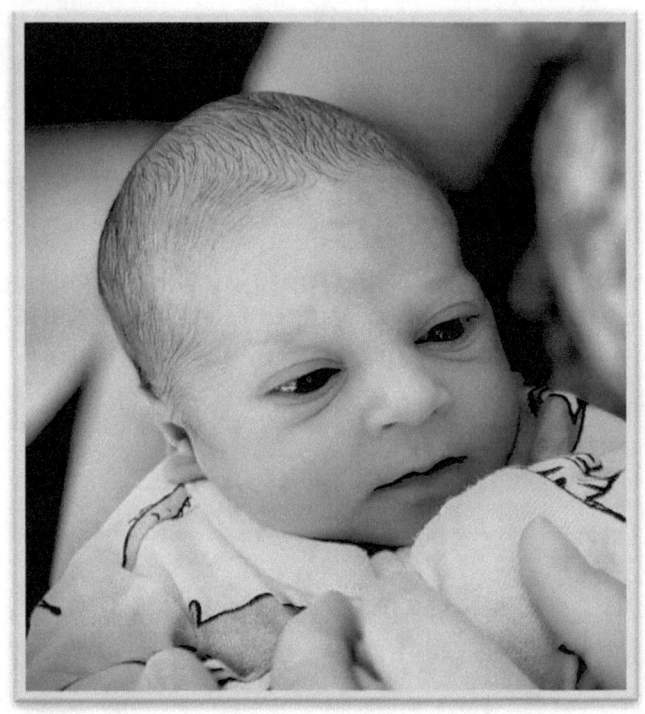

Once again we are blessed,
As we welcome Henry Samuel to our family.
And so, the story continues...

Through the Years

Debbie, Edna, Cindy

Cindy at the sandbox I made

Debbie at the piano

Debbie on the go-cart Dan Verina made

Me on my Italian scooter with Cindy on her scat-car

All together in our yard on Park Avenue, 1966

Daddy's girls

Our 25th Wedding Anniversary, September 10, 1975

Our 50th Wedding Anniversary, September 10, 2000

Epilogue

There will never be a final chapter as long as there is a tomorrow. Having passed my ninety-sixth birthday my thoughts towards the future are somewhat limited. Nonetheless, I try not to dwell on the past too much. I welcome each new day as a blessing. I have always considered myself the most fortunate of all my siblings. My darling and my two daughters have been the passion of my life. All my prayers have been answered, all my dreams have been fulfilled beyond any expectations. My only regret is that the one who contributed the most to my blessings is not here to share them with me. For over sixty years my loving wife was my soul partner, my inspiration, and my reason for living. Today I am enjoying the fruits of her love, sacrifices and dedication, and I know in my heart that's how she would have wanted it to be.

My prayers are that our future generations will continue with the wonderful traditions they have inherited. Thankfully, I am watching that materialize each day as our family continues to grow. The Fagnano offspring have all excelled in many different fields - arts, music, medicine, science, education, and all of them have a complete understanding of family values. My mother and father were the inspiration we all enjoyed. And although all the children, grandchildren and great-grandchildren have helped fill the vacuum left by the loss of my wife, brothers and sisters, my family memories remain precious and enduring and are a continuing source of comfort. It is my hope that this story of a struggling young family that endured life's triumphs and tragedies and kept their bonds strong, will now be an inspiration to others and a shining example of what faith and love can achieve.

I live each day with the words of the serenity prayer, "God grant me the serenity to accept the things I cannot change, the courage to change the things I can, and the wisdom to know the difference."

"There is no real ending. It's just the place where you leave the story."

Frank Herbert

An Ordinary Day, An Extraordinary Man

The day was much like any other day. The sky was bright blue, the sun was shining, the morning air was crisp. Our routine began as usual but something was different.

"I don't feel good", he said. "I feel strange". We made a call. And then, amidst a brief flurry of activity, life changed forever.

On September 18, 2024, Eugene Fagnano gently, quietly passed away.

On that very ordinary day, heaven welcomed an extraordinary man.

This book was a work of love, a work of art to which he was dedicated for more than a year. Every sentiment, every word and every photo was chosen with heartfelt deliberation. It represents all of what was dearest to him. Although he saw it through until his story was finished, he never saw the book in print.

He leaves a legacy for us to share with the hope that his message and his stories will continue in our minds and hearts and on the pages yet to be written.

He was dearly loved. He will be deeply missed. Still, though, we will fill our hearts not with grief but with gratitude for having had the blessing of sharing life with him. He taught us to recognize that a family is one of life's most precious gifts, one to be treasured more than wealth or fame. And we will continue living as he did always with the belief that above all, to love and be loved is truly the greatest joy on earth.

Together Forever

www.ingramcontent.com/pod-product-compliance
Lightning Source LLC
LaVergne TN
LVHW041707060526
838201LV00043B/622